International Library of Psychology
Philosophy and Scientific Method

Speculations

T. E. HULME

From a Bronze by Jacob Epstein

Speculations

ESSAYS ON HUMANISM AND
THE PHILOSOPHY OF ART

T. E. HULME

Edited by
HERBERT READ

With a Frontispiece and Foreword by
JACOB EPSTEIN

ROUTLEDGE & KEGAN PAUL
LONDON, HENLEY AND BOSTON

First published in 1924
by Routledge & Kegan Paul Ltd
39 Store Street,
London WC1E 7DD,
Broadway House,
Newtown Road,
Henley-on-Thames,
Oxon RG9 1EN and
9 Park Street,
Boston, Mass. 02108, U.S.A.
Second Edition 1936
Reprinted 1949, 1953, 1958, 1960, 1965, 1971 and 1977
Printed by Weatherby Woolnough,
Sanders Road, Wellingborough, Northants, NN8 4BX

ISBN 0 7100 3014 2

CONTENTS

FOREWORD

HULME was my very great friend, and what I can say about him is entirely personal.

What appealed to me particularly in him was the vigour and sincerity of his thought. He was capable of kicking a theory as well as a man downstairs when the occasion demanded. I always felt him to be my chief bulwark against malicious criticism. He was a man who had no regard for personal fame or notoriety, and he considered that his work lay entirely in the future. His whole life was a preparation for the task of interpretation which he had set himself. He would make reckless sacrifices to possess works of art which he could not really afford ; he bought not only my own works, but also those of Gaudier-Brzeska—and this long before Gaudier was well known.

Hulme was a terror to "fumistes" and charlatans of all kinds. His passion for the truth was uncontrolled.

I recall dozens of little personal things characteristic of the man—but particularly our first meeting. I was at work on the Wilde monument. Hulme immediately put his own construction on my work—turned it into some theory of projectiles. My sculpture only served to start the train of his thought. Abstract art had an extraordinary attraction for him : his own brain worked in that way.

At one time, in company with a group of " imagists," he composed some short poems with which, had he gone on, he would have made what would be called a literary " success." But this seemed to him too facile. Like Plato and Socrates, he drew the intellectual youth of his time around him. We have no one quite like him in England to-day.

JACOB EPSTEIN.

INTRODUCTION

THOMAS ERNEST HULME was born on the 16th September 1883, at Gratton Hall, Endon, North Staffordshire. He was educated at the High School, Newcastle-under-Lyme, and at St John's College, Cambridge. In March 1904 he was " sent down " from Cambridge, along with other undergraduates, for indulging in a brawl. He spent the next two years in London, studying in accordance with his own inclinations. In July 1906 he went to Canada, where he stayed three months. He returned to England for a few weeks, and early in 1907 he went to Brussels, where for seven months he taught English and learned French and German. When he came back to London he began definitely to study those subjects on which his interest was settling. In April 1911 he attended the Philosophical Congress at Bologna and stayed in Italy travelling for about three months. Early in 1912 he sought to return to Cambridge, and he was readmitted largely through the intervention of Professor Bergson, whose letter of recommendation on that occasion is some indication of the impression Hulme was already creating :—

SPECULATIONS

Je me fais un plaisir de certifier que je considère Mr T. E. Hulme comme un esprit d'une grande valeur. Il apporte, à l'étude des questions philosophiques, de rares qualités de finesse, de vigueur, et de pénétration. Ou je me trompe beaucoup, ou il est destiné à produire des œuvres intéressantes et importantes dans le domaine de la philosophie en général, et plus particulièrement peut-être dans celui de la philosophie de l'art.

Hulme's temperament was not one that could submit readily to an academic mould, and his university career was never completed in an orderly sense of the word. He left Cambridge shortly after his return and proceeded to Berlin, staying there for nine months and acquiring a wide knowledge of German philosophy and psychology. He then settled for a while in London, where his forceful personality and witty conversation began to form a group and to influence a generation. Then came the war. Hulme joined the Honourable Artillery Company and went to France shortly after Christmas 1914. He was wounded during the Spring of 1915 and upon recovery he was gazetted to the Royal Marine Artillery. He returned to the front late in 1915 and was killed near Nieuport on the 28th of September 1917. Hulme was a militarist by faith and acted upon his beliefs with a rare enthusiasm. Many notes, devoted to the technical problems of artillery practice and to strategy in general, testify to his serious interest ; and in the Military Notes, contributed to *The New Age* and *The Cambridge Magazine* under the *nom de guerre* of " North Staffs " during 1915 and 1916, he gave an intellectual defence of the militarist ideology which caused surprise not only to the militarists, to whom it was as strange as it might be deemed unnecessary, but also to the pacifists, who had regarded themselves as constituting a close corporation of the intelligentsia.

Meanwhile Hulme had not desisted from his more strictly intellectual pursuits. In 1913 he had published in a translation Bergson's *Introduction to Metaphysics,** and in 1916 appeared Sorel's *Reflections on Violence,*† translated by Hulme with a critical introduction. These two volumes, apart from the " Complete Poetical Works of T. E. Hulme," five poems,‡ printed in 1915 as an addendum to Mr Ezra Pound's *Ripostes,*§ and apart from various articles contributed to periodicals, make up the sum of Hulme's published work.

He left behind him a great mass of notebooks and manuscripts from which the present volume has been selected. From a " Notebook on Notebooks," which was among the material, it is possible to reconstruct some-

* London (Macmillan & Co. Ltd.).
† London (George Allen & Unwin Ltd.).
‡ See Appendix C.   § London (Elkin Mathews).

thing of Hulme's aims and methods of work. His plan was to keep :

(1) A daybook, which he always carried with him, and into which he entered every thought or observation as it occurred to him.

(2) A " corpus," into which as much of the daybook as on second sight seemed worthy was to be entered ; this to be indexed.

(3) When a general idea began to emerge from the accumulation of notes, then a new notebook or file was to be opened 'and all ideas that could be subsumed under that general idea were to be transferred.

(4) From this notebook the final work would be written.

Unfortunately this " Notebook on Note-books " shows signs of being one of the last things written by Hulme, and certainly the system was never put into complete operation. What existed when I began to edit his papers was a collection of hundreds of loose notes, varying in size from pieces of paper no bigger than a postage-stamp to complete folios of notes on one subject. Many of the notes had already been " written up " as articles in the *New Age ;* others had been made the subject of lectures ; the majority are mere indications of thoughts—key-words and key-phrases. But certain general ideas did exist, and at

least six works or series of works were taking
shape.   These were :

  I. Modern Theories of Art (see Appendix
      B).
 II. A General Introduction to the Phil-
      osophy of Bergson.
III. A book on Jacob Epstein and the
      Æsthetics of Sculpture.
 IV. A book on Expression and Style (the
      Psychology of Literature).
  V. A series of pamphlets on anti-human-
      ism, anti-romanticism, and pre-Re-
      naissance philosophy.
 VI. A philosophy or *Weltanschauung*, in
      an allegorical form.

Towards the first book there exist in manuscript various notes on modern æsthetics and
the essay on Bergson's Theory of Art now
published. The basis for the second book
had been formed as a series of four lectures on
the Philosophy of Bergson, which were delivered in London during 1913 ; from the notes
used for these lectures it has been possible
to piece together the essay now printed as
the Philosophy of Intensive Manifolds. The
book on Jacob Epstein was in an advanced
state of preparation at the time of Hulme's
death, but the manuscript perished with him.
Of the more original works he was engaged
on, the book on Expression and Style only

exists in the form of rudimentary notes—
mere indications to the author of a train of
thought associated with some image or expression. The series of pamphlets was planned
rather than executed : no doubt the essays
now printed as Humanism and the Religious
Attitude, and Romanticism and Classicism,
would have been issued in the series, which
was, however, to be a complete critical
examination of Renaissance ideologies and a
rehabilitation of pre-Renaissance philosophy.
There are indications of its trend and scope
in the Introduction to Sorel's *Reflections on
Violence*, reprinted as Appendix A. Lastly,
there was the work to which Hulme devoted
most of his thought and which he kept constantly in view. This was to be a personal
philosophy, cast into an allegorical form
perhaps analogous to Nietzsche's *Zarathustra*,
and having as its final object the destruction
of the idea that the world has unity, or that
anything can be described in words. The
notes for this book stretch over a considerable period—perhaps ten or fifteen years—
and are constantly rewritten and amended.
They were never given any final form, and
apart from the name Aphra, who was to be
the central figure, nothing of its allegorical
structure can be discerned. The more coherent fragments have been gathered together
in this volume under Hulme's own title
Cinders.

To attempt any exposition of the Speculations now " thrown to the lions " does not fall within my province. More than is usual in such writings, they speak for themselves. If Hulme had one foe exposed before all others to his consistent invective, it was obscurantism. He was not, by design, a systematic thinker. He was, in one sense at least, a poet : he preferred to see things in the emotional light of a metaphor rather than to reach reality through scientific analysis. His significance is none the less real ; he knew very certainly that we were at the end of a way of thought that had prevailed for four hundred years ; in this, and in his premonition of a more absolute philosophy of life, he had advanced the ideals of a new generation.

I wish to express my thanks to Mrs Kibblewhite and Miss Pattinson, who have supplied me with biographical material and helped me in other ways ; to Mr A. R. Orage, with whose assistance I began the work of editing ; and to Messrs George Allen & Unwin for permission to reprint the Introduction to Sorel's *Reflections on Violence.*

1924   HERBERT READ.

NOTE TO THE SECOND EDITION

In this new edition I have corrected a few misprints. In 1925 I published the *Notes on Language and Style* referred to on page xiv in *The Criterion* (Vol. III, page 485) and later they appeared as a pamphlet (University of Washington Chapbooks, No. 25, Seattle, 1929). It is not likely that any other material remains to be published.

HERBERT READ.

A PREFACE BY THE AUTHOR

The history of the philosophers we know, but who will write the history of the philosophic amateurs and readers? Who will tell us of the circulation of Descartes, who read the book and who understood it? Or do philosophers, like the mythical people on the island, take in each other's washing? Are they the only readers of each other's books? For I take it, a man who understands philosophy is inevitably irritated into writing it. The few who have learnt the jargon must repay themselves by employing it. A new philosophy is not like a new religion, a thing to be merely thankful for and accepted mutely by the faithful. It is more of the nature of food thrown to the lions; the pleasure lies in the fact that it can be devoured. It is food for the critics, and all readers of philosophy, I suppose, are critics, and not faithful ones waiting for the new gospel.

With this preface I offer my new kind of food to tickle the palate of the connoisseurs.

HUMANISM AND THE
RELIGIOUS ATTITUDE

HUMANISM AND THE RELIGIOUS ATTITUDE

A METHOD

ONE of the main achievements of the nineteenth century was the elaboration and
universal application of the principle of *continuity*. The destruction of this conception
is, on the contrary, an urgent necessity of the
present.

Originally urged only by the few, it has
spread—implicit in the popular conception of
evolution—till it has attained the status of a
category. We now absorb it unconsciously
from an environment already completely
soaked in it ; so that we regard it not as a
principle in the light of which certain regions
of fact can be conveniently ordered, but as
an inevitable constituent of reality itself.
When any fact seems to contradict this
principle, we are inclined to deny that the
fact really exists. We constantly tend to
think that the discontinuities in nature are
only *apparent*, and that a fuller investigation
would reveal the underlying continuity. This
shrinking from a *gap* or jump in nature has
developed to a degree which paralyses any
objective perception, and prejudices our see-

3

ing things as they really are. For an objective view of reality we must make use both of the categories of continuity and discontinuity. Our principal concern then at the present moment should be the re-establishment of the temper or disposition of mind which can look at a *gap* or chasm without shuddering.

I am not concerned in these notes, however, with gaps in nature, in the narrow sense of the word. I am thinking rather of general theories about the nature of reality. One of the results of the temper of mind I have just discussed is that any general theories of this kind which assert the existence of absolute gaps between one region of reality and another, are at once almost instinctively felt to be inadmissible. Now the method of criticism I wish to employ here is based on the fact that most of the errors in certain subjects spring from an almost instinctive attempt on our part to gloze over and disguise a particular *discontinuity* in the nature of reality. It was then necessary first of all to deal with the source of this instinctive behaviour, by pointing out the arbitrary character of the principle of continuity.

What is this Method ? It is only possible here to describe it quite abstractly, leaving the details till later. Certain regions of reality differ not relatively but absolutely. There exists between them a real discon-

tinuity.   As the mind looks on discontinuity
with horror it has attempted to exhibit these
opposed things as differing only in degree, as
if there is in reality a continuous scale leading
from one to the other.   From this springs a
whole mass of confused thinking in religion
and ethics.   If we first of all form a clear
conception of the nature of a discontinuity, of
a chasm, and form in ourselves the temper of
mind which can support this opposition without irritation, we shall then have in our hands
an instrument which may shatter all this
confused thinking, and enable us to form
accurate ideas on these subjects.   In this way
a flood of light may be thrown on old contro-
versies.

A necessary preliminary to this, however,
must be some account of the nature of the
particular absolute discontinuity that I want
to use.

In order to simplify matters, it may be
useful here to give the exposition a kind of
geometrical character.   Let us assume that
reality is divided into three regions, separated
from one another by absolute divisions, by
real discontinuities.   (1) The inorganic world,
of mathematical and physical science, (2) the
organic world, dealt with by biology, psychology and history, and (3) the world of
ethical and religious values.   Imagine these
three regions as three zones marked out
on a flat surface by two concentric circles.
The outer zone is the world of physics, the

inner that of religion and ethics, the intermediate one that of life. The outer and inner regions have certain characteristics in common. They have both an *absolute* character, and knowledge about them can legitimately be called absolute knowledge. The intermediate region of life is, on the other hand, essentially relative ; it is dealt with by *loose* sciences like biology, psychology and history. A muddy mixed zone then lies between two absolutes. To make the image a more faithful representation one would have to imagine the extreme zones partaking of the perfection of geometrical figures, while the middle zone was covered with some confused muddy substance.

I am afraid I shall have to abandon this model, for to make it represent faithfully what I want, I shall have to add a further complication. There must be an *absolute* division between each of the three regions, a kind of *chasm*. There must be no continuity, no bridge leading from one to the other. It is these *discontinuities* that I want to discuss here.

A convenient way of realising the nature of these divisions is to consider the movement away from materialism, at the end of the nineteenth century. In the middle period of the century, the predominant popular view entirely ignored the division between the inner and outer zones, and tended to treat them as one. There was no separating chasm and the two were muddled together. Vital phenomena were only extremely complicated forms of mechanical change. (Cf. Spencer's Biology and the entirely mechanical view involved in the definition of life as adaptation to environment.) Then you get the movement represented in very different ways by Nietzsche, Dilthey, and Bergson, which clearly recognised the chasm between the two worlds of life and matter. Vital events are not completely *determined* and mechanical. It will always be impossible to describe them completely in terms of the laws of physics. This was not merely a local reaction against a local false doctrine. It contained an original element. This movement made the immense step forward involved in treating life, almost for the first time, as a unity, as something positive, a kind of stream overflowing, or at any rate not entirely enclosed, in the boundaries of the physical and spatial world. " In dein Auge schaute ich, O Leben," etc.

So far so good. But the same movement that recognises the existence of the first absolute chasm (between the physical and the vital), proceeds to ignore the second, that between biology and the ethical, religious values. Having made this immense step away from materialism, it believes itself adequately equipped for a statement of all the *ideal* values. It does not distinguish

7

different levels of the non-material. All that is non-material, must it thinks be *vital*. The momentum of its escape from mechanism carries it on to the attempt to restate the whole of religion in terms of vitalism. This is ridiculous. Biology is not theology, nor can God be defined in terms of " life " or " progress." Modernism entirely misunderstands the nature of religion. But the last twenty years have produced masses of writing on this basis, and in as far as thought to-day is not materialistic, it tends to be exclusively of this kind.

It is easy to understand why the absolute division between the inorganic and the organic is so much more easily recognised than the second division. For the first falls easily into line with humanism, while the second breaks the whole Renaissance tradition.

It is necessary, however, that this second *absolute* difference should also be understood. It is necessary to realise that there is an absolute, and not a relative, difference between humanism (which we can take to be the highest expression of the vital), and the religious spirit. The *divine* is not *life* at its intensest. It contains in a way an almost *anti-vital* element ; quite different of course from the non-vital character of the outside physical region. The questions of Original Sin, of chastity, of the motives behind Buddhism, etc., all part of the very essence of the religious spirits, are quite incomprehensible

8

for humanism. The difference is seen perhaps most obviously in art. At the Renaissance, there were many pictures with religious subjects, but no religious art in the proper sense of the word. All the emotions expressed are perfectly human ones. Those who choose to think that religious emotion is only the highest form of the emotions that fall inside the humanist ideology, may call this religious art, but they will be wrong. When the intensity of the religious attitude finds proper expression in art, then you get a very different result. Such expression springs not from a delight in life but from a feeling for certain absolute values, which are entirely independent of vital things. The disgust with the trivial and accidental characteristics of living shapes, the searching after an austerity, a monumental stability and permanence, a perfection and rigidity, which vital things can never have, leads to the use of forms which can almost be called *geometrical*. (Cf. Byzantine, Egyptian and early Greek art.) If we think of physical science as represented by geometry, then instead of saying that the modern progress away from materialism has been from physics through vitalism to the absolute values of religion, we might say that it is from *geometry through life and back to geometry*. It certainly seems as if the extreme regions had resemblances not shared by the middle region. This is because they are both, in different ways, absolute.

SPECULATIONS

We can repeat this in a more summary form. Two sets of errors spring from the attempt to treat different regions of reality as if they were alike. (1) The attempt to introduce the *absolute* of mathematical physics into the essentially relative middle zone of life leads to the *mechanistic* view of the world. (2) The attempt to explain the *absolute* of religious and ethical values in terms of the categories appropriate to the essentially relative and non-absolute vital zone, leads to the entire misunderstanding of these values, and to the creation of a series of mixed or bastard phenomena, which will be the subject of these notes. (Cf. Romanticism in literature, Relativism in ethics, Idealism in philosophy, and Modernism in religion.)

To say that these bastard phenomena are the result of the shrinking from discontinuity would be an entirely inadequate account of the matter. They spring from a more positive cause, the inability of the prevailing ideology to understand the nature of this absolute. But they are certainly shaped by this instinctive effort to dig away at the edges of the precipice, which really separates two regions of reality, until it is transformed into a slope leading gradually from one to the other.

Romanticism, for example, confuses both human and divine things, by not clearly separating them. The main thing with which it can be reproached is that it blurs the clear outlines of human relations—whether in political thought or in the literary treatment of sex—by introducing in them the *Perfection* that properly belongs to the non-human.

The method I wish to pursue then is this. In dealing with these confused phenomena, to hold the real nature of the *absolute discontinuity* between vital and religious things constantly before the mind ; and thus to clearly separate those things, which are in reality separate. I believe this to be a very fertile method, and that it is possible by using it, not only to destroy all these bastard phenomena, but also to recover the real significance of many things which it seems absolutely impossible for the " modern " mind to understand.

A CRITIQUE OF SATISFACTION

ON an earlier page I made this assertion:
" In spite of its extreme diversity, all philosophy since the Renaissance is at bottom
the *same* philosophy. The family resemblance
is much greater than is generally supposed.
The obvious diversity is only that of the
various species of the same genus." It is
very difficult to see this when one is *inside*
this philosophy ; but if one looks at it from
the standpoint of another philosophy, it at
once becomes obvious. A parallel may make
this clearer. The change of sensibility which
has enabled us to regard Egyptian, Polynesian and Negro work, as *art* and not as
archæology has had a double effect. It has
made us realise that what we took to be the
necessary principles of æsthetic, constitute
in reality only a psychology of Renaissance
and Classical Art. At the same time, it has
made us realise the essential *unity* of these
latter arts. For we see that they both rest
on certain common pre-suppositions, of which
we only become conscious when we see them
denied by other arts. (Cf. the work of Riegl
on Byzantine art.) In the same way an
understanding of the religious philosophy

which preceded the Renaissance makes the essential unity of all philosophy since seem at once obvious. It all rests on the same conception of the nature of man, and exhibits the same inability to realise the meaning of the dogma of Original Sin. Our difficulty now, of course, is that we are really incapable of understanding how any other view but the humanistic could be seriously held by intelligent and emancipated men. To get over this difficulty I intend in later Notes to say a good deal about those comparatively unknown philosophers at the beginning of the Renaissance, who are exceptionally interesting from this point of view, because they exhibit clearly the transition from one ideology to the other. They at least were capable of understanding that an intelligent man might not be a humanist.

But we can leave this on one side. In order to explain this family likeness between all philosophers since the Renaissance, it is not necessary to state *specifically*, what the likeness consists in. The fact can perhaps be made comprehensible by the *manner* of its occurrence ; by stating the aspect or *department* in philosophy in which the resemblance occurs, without stating in detail what it is.

Philosophy is a surprising subject to the layman. It has all the appearance of an impersonal and exact science. It makes use of a terminology as abstruse as that of mathematics, and its method is so technical that he cannot follow it ; yet he can see for himself that it is not a science, or it would have the same solid growth as the other sciences. It ought surely to have arrived by now at results valid for everyone. But the scandal in philosophy of the contrast between apparently *impersonal*, scientific method, and its results—which are often so *personal*, that no one but their author accepts them—is obvious to everyone.

This scandal is so evident, that certain philosophers have endeavoured to end it, by *acknowledging* it. They say that the subject should renounce its claim to be a science, and should acknowledge itself to be, what it clearly is, a *Weltanschauung*, or expression of an attitude towards the world. The personal element in it would then be legitimate.

This I now believe to be a false solution.

What is the right solution ? To recognise that actual Philosophy is not a pure but a *mixed* subject. It results from a confusion between two subjects which stand in no essential or necessary relation to each other, though they may be combined together for a certain practical end. One of these subjects is a science, the other not. The scientific element in philosophy is a difficult investigation into the relations between certain very abstract categories. Though the subject

14

matter is abstract, the method employed
should be as purely scientific and impersonal
as that of mathematics.

Mixed up with this is the function which
philosophy has assumed of acting as a pale
substitute for religion. It is concerned here
with matters like the nature and destiny of
man, his place in the universe, etc., all matters ·
which would, as treated, fit very well into a
personal Weltanschauung. Here the word
" standpoint " may legitimately be used,
though it is quite illegitimate in the scientific
part of philosophy.

The two elements are mixed after this
fashion. The machinery elaborated by the
first element in philosophy is used to further
the aims of the second. Put very crudely
these aims make it first of all necessary that
the world should be shown to be in *reality*
very different from what it *appears* to be.
It must be moulded " nearer to the heart's
desire." By the aid of his technical equipment—the result of the first element—the
philosopher is able to disintegrate the solid
structure of the world as it appears to common
sense. In the last chapter, in his " conclusions," he presents us with his reconstructed
world ; with the world as it is in *reality*.
Consider the nature of this second feature for a
moment. The philosopher undertakes to show
that the world is other than it appears to me ;
and as he takes the trouble to prove this, we
should expect to find that consciously or

unconsciously the *final* picture he presents
will to some degree or other *satisfy* him.

It is these final pictures that make it true
to say that there is a family resemblance
between all philosophers since the Renaissance. Though the pictures are as different
as can be, yet curiously enough they are all
satisfactory for approximately the same
reasons. The *final* pictures they present of
man's relation to the world all conform to
the same probably unconscious *standards* or
canons of what is *satisfying*. It would be
more accurate to say that it is the similarity
of these *canons* that constitutes the unity of
modern philosophy. If we think, then, of
philosophy as divided into a *scientific*, and a
more *personal* part, we may say that the
various systems agree where they might have
been expected to differ—and disagree where
they ought to have been impersonal ; they
vary where no variation should have been
possible—in the scientific part.

It should be noticed that these canons of
satisfaction are quite unconscious. The philosophers share a view of what would be a
satisfying destiny for man, which they take
over from the Renaissance. They are all
satisfied with certain conceptions of the relation of man to the world. These *conclusions*
are never questioned in this respect. Their
truth may be questioned, but never their

satisfactoriness. This ought to be questioned. This is what I mean by a *critique of satisfaction*. When Croce, for example, finishes up with the final world-picture of the "legitimate" *mystery of infinite progress and the infinite perfectibility of man*—I at once want to point out that not only is this not true, but, what is even more important, if true, such a shallow conception would be quite unworthy of the emotion he feels towards it.

These *canons of satisfaction*, which are the results of an entirely uncritical humanism, should be subject to a *critique*. This is a special subject, having no connection with philosophy. I hope to be able to show that it is a real and complicated subject inside the limits of which detailed investigation is possible, by the aid of a refined and subtle analysis.

This is a very rough account of the matter. To make it convincing, it is first of all necessary to examine in more detail the nature of the alleged confusion in actual philosophy. In pointing out that the scientific part of the subject was actually used to serve very human ends, I did not want to imply any scepticism as to the possibility of a really scientific philosophy. I do not mean what Nietzsche meant when he said, "Do not speculate as to whether what a philosopher says is true, but ask how he came to think it true." This form of scepticism I hold to be just fashionable rubbish. Pure philosophy ought to be, and may be, entirely objective and scientific.

The best account I know of the sense in which Philosophy may be a science is that given by Husserl in *Logos*, 1911—" Philosophie als strenge Wissenschaft." One definition would be that of philosophy as the *science of what is possible* as contrasted with the *science of what is*—something similar to what Meinong means by *Gegenstandtheorie*. I have no space here to explain what is meant by these definitions. All that it is necessary to keep in mind here is that Philosophy may be a patient investigation into entities, which although they are abstract, may yet be investigated by methods as objective as those of physical science. There are then two distinct subjects :—

(L.) Pure Philosophy.

(H.) This should be the critique of satisfaction ; but instead it is, as a matter of fact, an entirely uncritical acceptance of Humanist views of man's nature, and destiny.

These two ought to be clearly separated. What you actually do get in philosophy, is a presentment of these humanist ideas, with a tremendous and overwhelming appearance of being *impersonal objective* science. You get something perfectly human and arbitrary cloaked in a scientific vocabulary. Instead of H or L, you get L(h) where the (h) is the really important factor. H moves in the stiff armour of L. Something quite *human* but with quite *inhumanly* sharpened weapons.

I remember being completely overawed by the vocabulary and scientific method of the various philosophers of the Marburg School, and in particular by Herman Cohen's " Logik der reinen Erkenntniss." But one day, hearing Cohen lecture on religion, where his views are, as is well known, entirely sectarian, I realised very easily that the overwhelming and elaborate method only served to express a perfectly simple and fallible human attitude.

This was very exhilarating and enlightening. One could at last stand free, disentangled from the influence of their paralysing and elaborate method. For what was true of their work in religion was also true elsewhere. It becomes possible to see a good deal of Cohen's work as the rigid, scientific expression of an attitude that is neither rigid nor scientific, but sometimes romantic, and always humanist. One can illustrate the effect of such work on the mind by this parallel. A man might be clothed in armour so complicated and elaborate, that to an inhabitant of another planet who had never seen armour before, he might seem like some entirely impersonal and omnipotent mechanical force. But if he saw the armour running after a lady or eating tarts in the pantry, he would realise at once, that it was not a godlike or mechanical force, but an ordinary human being extraordinarily armed. In the pantry, the essence of the phenomena is not *arms, but the man.*

When you have recovered from the precision and refinement of the *method* in such philosophers, you will be able to recognise the frequent vulgarity of their *conclusions.* It is possible to combine extreme subtlety in the one, with exceeding commonplaceness in the other.

If you ask what corresponds to the pantry which betrayed the man in armour, I should answer that it was the *last* chapters of the philosophers in which they express their conception of the world as it really is, and so incidentally expose the things with which they are satisfied. How magnificently they may have been clad before, they come out naked here !

This emancipation is, however, only a secondary matter. What I wish to emphasise here is the corrective, the *complexity* of this supposed " Critique of Satisfaction." By the complexity of this subject, I mean amongst other things, the many possible different ideals, or *canons of satisfaction.* It is difficult to make the people I am attacking realise this, because they always assume automatically, that all *ideals* must be *one* ideal, and that everything that is not sceptical materialism, must be some form of *humanism*. One of the causes of this assumption can be easily dealt with. The difficulty is exactly parallel to the difficulty the scientific materialists of the last century used to experience in realising that metaphysics was a real region of knowledge.

One can put the parallel clearly.

(1) The *Naturalists* refused to recognise metaphysical knowledge because

(2) They themselves were under the influence of an *unconscious metaphysic* which consisted in

(3) Taking physical science as the only possible *type* of real knowledge.

The parallel is :—

(1) The *Humanists* would refuse to recognise the existence of a subject like the critique of satisfaction because

(2) They themselves are under the influence of an *unconscious critique* of this kind which consists in

(3) Taking the satisfaction and consolation which can be obtained from humanist idealism, and its view of man, as the only possible *type* of satisfaction.

This removes an *a priori* objection to the

subject. What then finally is the nature of the subject ?

. . . . . .

What actually would be the subject matter of a *Critique of Satisfaction ?*

Very roughly, the *Sphere of Religion.* But to say this at once calls up a conception different from the one I am driving at.

It is on the whole correct to say that while Ethics is concerned with certain absolute values, and has nothing to do with questions of *existence*, that Religion fills in this gap by its assertion of what Höffding calls the characteristic axiom of religion : the "*conservation of* values." It gives us the assurance that values are in some way permanent.

This is in a sense correct, in that it gives us so to speak the *boundaries* of the subject. But it is entirely empty. To get at the motive forces one would have to start in an entirely different way. I should say that the starting point for the religious attitude was always the kind of discussion you find in Pascal (*Fragment* 139. Brunschvig edition) ; and that is exactly what I mean by a *Critique of Satisfaction.* You get exactly similar discussion in the Buddhist books (entirely misunderstood of course by their translators and editors). My point is that this is a *separate* subject. It is *not* philosophy, *nor* is it *psychology*. Always the subject is the "*Vanity of desire*" but it is *not* desire merely as a psychological entity. And it is this

22

special region of knowledge, marked out from all other spheres of knowledge, and absolutely and entirely *misunderstood* by the moderns, that I have baptized for the purpose of this Note only with the somewhat grotesque title of the *Critique of Satisfaction*.

FALSE CATEGORIES

I HAVE been concerned so far with the mixed nature of Philosophy, and the necessity of analysing it into *Scientific* philosophy and *Weltanschauung*. I now want to offer (1) a more detailed account of the *existence* of these two elements ; and (2) a discussion of the consequences of this separation.

(1) A *Weltanschauung* is by no means necessarily connected with a philosophy. The effort to find some " interpretation of life," to solve what it feels to be the riddle of existence, is obviously a permanent characteristic of the human mind. It may find expression not only in philosophy, however, but in literature ; where in a relatively formless way attempts may be made to deal with the relation of man to the world, and with all those questions, the answers to which used to be designated as *Wisdom*.

But though it can thus exist quite independently of philosophy, yet a *Weltanschauung*, a particular view of the relation of man to existence, always tends to lose its independent status for this reason—the people who are under its influence want to *fix* it, to make it seem not so much a particular *attitude* as a *necessary* fact. They then en-

24

deavour, by expressing it in the elaborately worked out categories of a metaphysic, to give it a universal validity. Philosophy in this way provides a conceptual clothing for the interpretation of life current in any particular period. But the interpretation of life should always be distinguished from the refined organisation of concepts by which it has been expressed.

This process can be illustrated more concretely by taking a definite period. Consider the most obvious example of the emergence of a new *Weltanschauung*—the Renaissance. You get at that time the appearance of a new attitude which can be most broadly described as an attitude of acceptance to life, as opposed to an attitude of renunciation. As a consequence of this, there emerges a new interest in man and his relationship to his environment. With this goes an increasing interest in character and *personality* for its own sake, which makes autobiographies such as that of Cellini possible for the first time. An autobiography for its own sake would have been inconceivable before.

Though these are platitudes, yet their real significance is entirely missed by people who do not see this change as a change from one *possible* attitude to another, but as a kind of discovery, like that of gravitation. They thus fail to realise the possibility of a change in the contrary direction, and also to understand the real nature of such *attitudes*.

25

SPECULATIONS

When this new *attitude* became firmly established, men sought to make it seem *objective* and *necessary* by giving it a philosophical setting, exactly as in the case of the religious attitude which had preceded it. This was a need actually felt by many men of the Renaissance. One has only to read of the reception given to the philosophers who attempted to ground the new attitude on a theory of the nature of things . . . of the travels of Bruno, and the recorded eagerness of the men to whom he talked at a banquet in Westminster.

To make this clear, I shall later on attempt to describe the working out of the process in the sixteenth and seventeenth centuries. It is interesting to see how the conceptual expression of the new attitude was affected by the influence of the physics of Galileo, and the revived knowledge of Stoicism, to name only two things. It becomes possible to see the whole period as very much more of a unity than it appears superficially, when the existence of the new *attitude* as the driving force behind very diverse phenomena has once been realised. This is, of course, a process which is repeated whenever the general " interpretation of life " changes. At the *end* of such periods you get a constant phenomenon, the unsystematic philosopher. When the *Weltanschauung*, the interpretation of life, changes, the values expressed by the elaborate and subtle conceptual form of a

developed philosophy no longer fit the changed
conditions. You then get philosophers of the
type of Marcus Aurelius, who express the new
attitude in a more personal, literary, and
unsystematic way. Perhaps Marcus Aurelius
is not a good example of this type, for behind
his unsystematic expression lay a certain
remnant of the Stoic principles. A more
perfect example of the type is Montaigne,
coming after the decay of the scholastic
system. There are people at the present day
who look for a philosophy of this character,
who desire an "interpretation of life" without the elaborate conceptual system of the
older philosophy. "Their eyes are directed
with great earnestness on the Riddle of Life,
but they despair of solving it by a universally
valid metaphysic." The fact that philosophy has always contained this element of
Weltanschauung can be illustrated by some
examples of the use of the word. Justin
called Christianity a philosophy, for he claimed
that it had solved all the riddles with which
philosophy had busied itself. Minucius Felix
spoke of philosophy as perfected in Christianity . . . eternal truths about God, human
responsibility and immortality, which are
grounded on Reason, and can be proved
through it. . . . For Porphyrios the motive
and end of philosophy was the salvation of
the soul . . . and even Böhme called his
own life-work, a holy philosophy.

Such has been, in fact, the relation between

SPECULATIONS

Weltanschauung and Pure Philosophy. What *ought* to be the character of this relation ?

(2) As typical of the demand for a truly scientific philosophy, we can take the article by Edmund Husserl I cited previously, and in England various lectures and essays of Bertrand Russell. These two writers have most clearly insisted on the necessity for an absolute separation between *Pure* Philosophy and *Weltanschauung*.

RUSSELL : " It is from science rather than from religion and ethics that philosophy ought to draw its inspiration." He cites Spinoza as a philosopher whose value lies almost entirely in the second element. " We do not go to him for any metaphysical theory as to the nature of the world. What is valuable in him is the indication of a new way of feeling towards the world." His conclusion is " the adoption of the scientific method in philosophy compels us to abandon the hope of solving the more ambitious and humanly interesting problems of traditional philosophy."

HUSSERL : " Es treten also scharf auseinander : Weltanschauungs Philosophie und wissenschaftliche Philosophie, als zwei in gewisser Weise auf einander bezogene aber nicht zu *vermengenden* Ideen. . . ." The first is *not* the imperfect anticipation of the second. . . . Any combination or *compromise* between these two subjects must be rejected. . . . *Weltanschauung* philosophy must give up all pretence to be scientific.

While I entirely agree with what they say as to the possibility of a purely *scientific* philosophy and the necessity for a clear separation between that and a *Weltanschauung*, yet for the purpose of my argument in this Notebook I must lay emphasis on a different aspect of this separation. They insist on a clear separation, because they wish to free the scientific element in philosophy from bad influence of the other. They want the *Weltanschauung* separated from philosophy because they think it has often injuriously affected the scientific part of the subject. I, on the contrary, want it separated because I think it also forms part of a *separate* subject, which has in reality no connection with philosophy.

My interest, then, is a different one, and I examine what they have to say on the separation from a different point of view. I find that while what they say is satisfactory in its description of the nature of a purely scientific philosophy, it is extremely unsatisfactory in what it has to say about the nature of a *Weltanschauung*. After the remarkably clear exposition of the scientific element, one expects but does not find a similarly clear explanation of the other element.

What Mr Russell has to say on the subject in " A Free Man's Worship " is so extremely commonplace, and is expressed in such a painful piece of false and sickly rhetoric, that I have not patience to deal with it here.

Husserl, though he is better than this, is not very satisfactory. " A *Weltanschauung* should be the highest possible exaltation of the life and culture of the period. The word ' Wisdom ' taken in its widest sense comes to mean the most perfect possible development of the idea of Humanity. Personality is to be developed to the greatest intensity in a many-sided activity—the result will be a *philosopher* in the original sense of the word . . . while science is impersonal . . . a *Weltanschauung* can only spring from the highest possible development of personality."

The emphasis laid on the word *personality* at once shows us that instead of the complicated subject it really is, *Weltanschauung* philosophy is for Husserl, as it is for most moderns, merely an uncritical humanism.

How does it come about that the writers who show such subtlety in the scientific part of the subject, exhibit when they come to the subjects, which I proposed to deal with by a Critique of Satisfaction, such entirely uncritical and naïve crudity ? What is the reason for this commonplace, unquestioning acceptance of humanist ideas ?

In general, perhaps, for some reason of this kind. The ordinary citizen reasons correctly, without necessarily being aware that the cogency of a chain of reasoning depends on the fact that it approximates to certain standards or *canons* of implication. The philosophers, in their *conclusions,* in the region of *Weltan-schauung* are exactly in the position of the citizen in regard to logic. They are moved by certain unconscious *canons* of satisfaction. But while this was legitimate in the case of logic, it is not legitimate here, for the *canons* of satisfaction are not inevitable norms, like those of logic. The humanist *canons* are, I think, demonstrably false. But it is difficult to make these people realise that the canons are *false,* for they do not yet recognise that they exist. Now we only become conscious of such hidden presuppositions when they are *denied ;* just as we become conscious of the existence of air, when we breathe something that is not air. It is possible to destroy this *naïveté* about the subject by an historical investigation of the varied ideals of a *satis-factory* position of man that have as a matter of fact been held. I shall deal with this matter later. For the moment, I want to try to get at the *Critique of Satisfaction,* by the *direct method.*

My notes here will necessarily be rather disjointed ; but I only intend to suggest the kind of subject matter to be dealt with by such a Critique.

This subject matter was, I asserted in my last Note, that of religion ; but in a very radical sense. Most explanations of the religious attitude deal with the *consequences* of that attitude rather than with the attitude itself ; they are concerned more than they ought to be with the statements about the ultimate nature of things, which it, as it were, projects out from itself. The only fertile method is to start at the real root of the subject, with reflections on the nature of the " satisfying." You then get at a unique subject, with a special structure ; of such a nature, that the reasonings it employs have real cogency and real effect on action.

You get thus to the actual source of religion. Moreover, it might be pointed out here, that the difficulty about religion at the present day, is not so much the difficulty of believing the statements it makes about the nature of the world, as the difficulty of understanding *how if true* these statements can be satisfactory.

Put very crudely, the question from which everything here springs is then " what is finally *satisfying ?* "

For the purpose of this discussion, I assume the truth of the statement I made in an earlier note : " The whole subject has been confused by the failure to recognise the *gap* between the regions of vital and human things, and that of the *absolute* values of ethics and religion. We introduce into human things the *Perfection* that properly belongs only to the divine, and thus confuse both human and divine things by not clearly

32

separating them." To illustrate the position, imagine a man situated at a point in a plane, from which roads radiate in various directions. Let this be the plane of actual existence. We place *Perfection* where it should not be—on this human plane. As we are painfully aware that nothing *actual* can be *perfect*, we imagine the perfection to be not where we are, but some distance along one of the roads. This is the essence of all Romanticism. Most frequently, in literature, at any rate, we imagine an impossible *perfection* along the road of sex ; but anyone can name the other roads for himself. The abolition of some discipline and restriction would enable us, we imagine, to progress along one of these roads. The fundamental error is that of placing Perfection in *humanity*, thus giving rise to that bastard thing Personality, and all the bunkum that follows from it.

For the moment, however, I am not concerned with the errors introduced into *human* things by this confusion of regions which should be separated, but with the falsification of the *divine*.

If we continue to look with satisfaction along these roads, we shall always be unable to understand the religious attitude. The necessary preliminary *preparation* for such an understanding is a realisation that satisfaction is to be found along none of these roads.

The effect of this necessary *preparation* is to force the mind back on the centre, by the closing of all the roads *on* the plane. No " meaning " can be given to the existing world, such as philosophers are accustomed to give in their last chapters. To each conclusion one asks, " In what way is that *satisfying ?* " The mind is forced back along every line in the plane, back on the centre. What is the result ? To continue the rather comic metaphor, we may say the result is that which follows the snake eating its own tail, an *infinite* straight line *perpendicular* to the plane.

In other words, you get the religious attitude ; where things are separated which ought to be separated, and Perfection is not illegitimately introduced on the plane of human things.

It is the closing of all the roads, this realisation of the *tragic* significance of life, which makes it legitimate to call all other attitudes shallow. Such a realisation has formed the basis of all the great religions, and is most conveniently remembered by the symbol of the *wheel*. This symbol of the futility of existence is absolutely lost to the modern world, nor can it be recovered without great difficulty.

One modern method of disguising the issue should be noticed. In November 1829, a tragic date for those who see with regret the establishment of a lasting and devastating stupidity, Goethe—in answer to Eckermann's remark that human thought and action seemed to repeat itself, going round in a circle—said : " *No, it is not a circle, it is a spiral.*" You disguise the wheel by making it run up an inclined plane ; it then becomes " Progress," which is the modern substitute for religion.

I ought here to point out that these crude conceptions are designed only to suggest the subject-matter, which properly developed has no connection with philosophy. And just as exceeding refinement and subtlety in pure philosophy may have been combined with exceeding commonplaceness in this subject, so the reverse of this is also true. Even a cobbler may on this subject exhibit a refined sensibility, and yet be incapable of philosophic thought.

This crude discussion about the wheel must sound entirely unreal to the humanist. The direct method of approval will not do for propaganda purposes. Fortunately a more indirect method is open to us. We can make a preliminary attempt to shake the humanist *naïveté* by the historical method.

HISTORY

THE greater part of what I have to say here will be taken up by an analysis of the history of ideas at the *Renaissance.* A proper understanding of the Renaissance seems to me to be the most pressing necessity of thought at the present moment. It would be quite impossible to discuss the subjects of these Notes, without continual use of the historical method. I entirely agree, then, with Savigny that " history is the only true way to attain a knowledge of our own condition." When I say I agree with Savigny's phrase, I am, however, attributing an entirely different meaning to the words. As actually used in 1815, they were an incident in the dispute as to the nature of the ideal sciences—economics, law, ethics, etc. Are they capable of a theoretical foundation like geometry, or are the principles they involve merely expressions of the conditions at a given moment in history ? While the eighteenth century had attempted to change legal institutions in accordance with the Rights of Man deduced from theoretical principles, Savigny was opposing to these the entirely historical foundation of jurisprudence. This scepticism of the historical school on the question of principle has now been vanquished in every subject. I approve of this victory ;

in what sense then do I think Savigny's words true ?

I think that history is necessary in order to *emancipate* the individual from the influence of certain *pseudo-categories*. We are all of us under the influence of a number of abstract ideas, of which we are as a matter of fact unconscious. We do not see them, but see other things *through* them. In order that the kind of discussion about " satisfaction " which I want may be carried on, it is first of all necessary to rob certain ideas of their status of categories. This is a difficult operation. Fortunately, however, all such " attitudes " and ideologies have a gradual growth. The rare type of historical intelligence which investigates their origins can help us considerably. Just as a knowledge of the colours extended and separated in the spectrum enables us to distinguish the feebler colours confused together in shadows, so a knowledge of these ideas, as it were *objectified*, and *extended* in history enables us to perceive them hidden in our own minds. Once they have been brought to the surface of the mind, they lose their *inevitable* character. They are no longer categories. We have lost our *naïveté*. Provided that we have a great enough length of history at our disposal, we then always vaccinate ourselves against the possibility of harbouring false categories. For in a couple of thousand years the confused human mind works itself out clearly into all the separate attitudes it is possible for it to assume. Humanity ought therefore always to carry with it a library of a thousand years as a balancing pole.

The application of the historical method to the present subject is this : It is possible by examining the history of the Renaissance, to destroy in the mind of the humanist, the conviction that his own attitude is the *inevitable* attitude of the emancipated and instructed man.

We may not be able to convince him that the religious attitude is the right one, but we can at least destroy the *naïveté* of his canons of *satisfaction*.

NEO-REALISM

HAVING lived at Cambridge at various times during the last ten years, I have naturally always known that the only philosophical movement of any importance in England, is that which is derived from the writings of Mr G. E. Moore. I now find these writings extremely lucid and persuasive, yet for years was entirely unable to understand in what lay their value. It was not so much that I did not agree with what was said, as that I was entirely unable to see how any meaning could be attached to some of its main contentions. I give examples of these contentions later on.

A few years ago I came across similar views differently expressed in the work of Husserl and his followers. I then began for the first time, if not to agree with these views, at least to understand how they came to be held. It is not that the Germans are better or more lucid than Mr Moore—that is very far from being the case. The reason is entirely personal; but it seems to me worth while explaining, for my difficulties are at least the *typical* difficulties of the dilettante. It would be no exaggeration, I think, to assert that all English amateurs in philosophy are, as it were, *racially* empiric and nominalist; there is their hereditary endowment. And so long as their interest in the subject is a dilettante one they are unlikely to find much meaning in philosophers who are intellectualist and *realist*. For the reading of the dilettante in philosophy, though it may be extensive and enthusiastic, always proceeds along easy slopes. As he only reads what he finds interesting, the only arguments he is likely to come into close contact with—or, at any rate, into that extremely close contact which is necessary for the understanding of disputed points in this subject—will be those which approximate to its own position. If his own mental make-up, at a given moment be A, his only chance of understanding an opposed position B will be in the case when the detailed exposition of B as b_1, b_2, b_3, a, contains one element (a) which he can lay hold of. This is the only way in which he will ever obtain a foothold. From that he may gradually proceed to understand the rest. But without that he would never exhibit the concentration of mind necessary to grasp the meaning of an argument which he rejects. There is, you perceive, nothing very admirable about this type of mind. There is, however, something to be said for it. In the end it probably gets everywhere, though as it always shrinks from precipices, and proceeds along easy-slopes, through a hundred gradations of a_1, a_2, a_3, before it gets from A to B—it will always require an unlimited time. As its interests change, it may read many different parts of the same book, at long intervals, until finally as the result of many enthusiasms, it has read the whole. This blind following of interest along long and intricate paths may indirectly approximate to the results which concentration achieves directly. At any rate, I prefer people who feel a *resistance* to opinion. Except for the gifted few, this may be the best method to pursue in philosophy up to forty. It might be argued that a concentrated direct study of such matters should be postponed to this time, when a man really has prejudices to be moulded. There is, perhaps, more chance of getting *shape* out of stone than out of undergraduate plasticine. That this is a fair analysis of that very widespread phenomenon " Superficial thinking," we can verify by examining our own procedure in these matters. It, at any rate, enables me to explain my own difficulties. When, with entirely empirical and nominalist prejudices, I read Moore and Russell, there was no foothold for me ; they dealt with logic and ethics, and holding, as I did, entirely relativist views about both, I naturally found nothing familiar from which I might have started to understand the rest. The Germans I mentioned were useful in this way ; they made the intellectualist, non-empirical method comprehensible to me, by enlarging its scope —applying it not only to logic and ethics, but to things which at the time did interest me. This provided me with the required foothold. When I had seen in these further subjects the possibility of the *rationalist, non-empirical* method, I began to see that it was this method which formed the basis of the writing on logic and ethics which I had before found incomprehensible.

This will be then the order of my argument here. I give certain views of the Realists, which I at one time found incomprehensible. When I began to see for the first time the possibility of a non-empirical type of knowledge, the incomprehensibility of these views disappeared. In this Note I am, however, not concerned with their realism, but with the attitude (the assumption of this type of knowledge) from which the realism and its attendant difficulties spring.

In this kind of knowledge, the same type of non-empirical reasoning is possible as in geometry ; and its subject-matter stands in much the same relation to the concepts we generally, but falsely, call mental, that geometry does to physical matter. When the only admitted kind of knowledge is empirical, the only type of explanation considered legitimately is that which reduces all the " higher " concepts to combinations of more elementary ones. It is for this reason that I deal here with a subject that does not seem to have much relation to the general argument. For this false conception of the nature of " explanation " prejudices the understanding of the " Critique of Satisfaction."

It is first of all necessary before entering on this subject to destroy prejudices springing from empiricism, which tend to make us think certain concepts unreal.

The first difficulty was that Moore's only book was about Ethics. To anyone taking a thoroughly sceptical and relativist view of this subject, the whole discussion would quite wrongly appear almost entirely verbal. The only solution to this difficulty is the gradual realisation of the fact that there are objective things in Ethics, and this seems to me the only solution. I do not think any argument on the matter would have any effect unless a man had by some change in himself come to see that ethics was a real subject.

The principal difficulty, however, is the importance the Neo-Realists seem to attach to *language*. Mr Russell says, " That all sound philosophy should begin with an analysis of propositions is a truth too evident perhaps to demand a proof." " The question whether all propositions are reducible to the subject predicate form is one of fundamental importance to all philosophy."

" Even amongst philosophers we may say, broadly, that only those universals which are named by adjectives or substantives have been much or often recognised, while those named by verbs and propositions have been usually overlooked. . . . This omission has had a very great effect upon philosophy ;

it is hardly too much to say, that most meta-physics, since Spinoza, has been largely de-termined by it."

Mr G. E. Moore in an article on the " Nature of Judgment."* " It seems necessary, then, to regard the world as formed of concepts . . . which cannot be regarded as abstractions either for things or ideas . . . since both alike can, if anything be true of them, be comprised of nothing but concepts . . . an existent is seen to be nothing but a concept or complex of concepts standing in a unique relation to the concept of existence."

Such assertions must seem meaningless to the nominalist and empiricist. The whole thing seems to him to be a new kind of scholasticism. He cannot understand how the study of such an apparently relative and trivial thing as the nature of propositions, the study of the accidental characteristics of human speech, should be an indispensable preliminary to philosophy.

The first step towards making the matter intelligible is to note the use of the word *human*. A proposition in the sense used in the above quotation is not something relative to the *human*. " A proposition . . . does not itself contain words . . . it contains the entities indicated by words." One recalls Bolzano's " Sentences in themselves." Logic, then, does *not* deal with the laws of human

* This article is now reprinted in Dr Moore's *Philosophical Studies* (International Library of Psychology, 1922).

thought but with these quite *objective* sentences. In this way the anthropomorphism which underlies certain views of logic is got rid of. Similarly, ethics can be exhibited as an objective science, and is also purified from anthropomorphism.

All these subjects are thus placed on an entirely objective basis, and do not in the least depend on the human mind. The entities which form the subject-matter of these sciences are neither physical nor mental, they " subsist." They are dealt with by an investigation that is *not* empirical. Statements can be made about them whose truth does not depend on experience. When the empirical prejudice has been got rid of, it becomes possible to think of certain " higher " concepts, those of the good, of love, etc., as, at the same time, *simple*, and not necessarily to be analysed into more *elementary* (generally sensual) elements.

To make this intelligible, two things must be further discussed : (1) the possibility of this non-empirical knowledge ; (2) what is meant by saying that these entities are neither physical nor mental, but *subsist ?*

A PROGRAMME

THE main argument of these pages is of an *abstract* character ; it is concerned with certain ideas which lie so much in the centre of our minds, that we quite falsely regard them as having the nature of categories. More particularly, I am concerned with two opposed conceptions of the nature of man, which in reality lie at the root of our more concrete beliefs — the Religious and the Humanist.

It would perhaps have been better to have avoided the word religious, as that to the " emancipated " man at once suggests something exotic, or mystical, or some sentimental reaction. I am not, however, concerned so much with religion, as with the attitude, the " way of thinking," the categories, from which a religion springs, and which often survive it. While this attitude tends to find expression in myth, it is independent of myth ; it is, however, much more intimately connected with dogma. For the purposes of this discussion, the bare minimum without any expression in religion is sufficient, the abstract categories alone. I want to emphasise that this attitude is a possible one for the " emancipated " and " reasonable " man at this moment. I use the word religious, because as in the past the attitude

46

has been the source of most religions, the word remains convenient.

A.—The Religious attitude : (1) Its first postulate is the impossibility I discussed earlier, of expressing the absolute values of religion and ethics in terms of the essentially relative categories of life. . . . Ethical values are *not* relative to human desires and feelings, but absolute and objective. . . . Religion supplements this . . . by its conception of *Perfection*.

(2) In the light of these absolute values, man himself is judged to be essentially limited and imperfect. He is endowed with Original Sin. While he can occasionally accomplish acts which partake of perfection, he can never himself *be* perfect. Certain secondary results in regard to ordinary human action in society follow from this. A man is essentially bad, he can only accomplish anything of value by discipline—ethical and political. Order is thus not merely negative, but creative and liberating. Institutions are necessary.

B.—The Humanist attitude : When a sense of the reality of these absolute values is lacking, you get a refusal to believe any longer in the radical imperfection of either Man or Nature. This develops logically into the belief that life is the source and measure of all values, and that man is fundamentally good. Instead, then, of

Man (radically imperfect) . . . apprehending . . . Perfection,—

you get the second term (now entirely

47

misunderstood) illegitimately introduced inside the first. This leads to a complete change
in all values. The problem of evil disappears,
the conception of sin loses all meaning. Man
may be that bastard thing, " a harmonious
character." Under ideal conditions, everything of value will spring spontaneously
from free " personalities." If nothing good
seems to appear spontaneously now, that is
because of external restrictions and obstacles.
Our political ideal should be the removal of
everything that checks the " spontaneous
growth of personality." Progress is thus
possible, and order is a merely negative
conception.

The errors which follow from this confusion
of things which ought to be kept separate
are of two kinds. The true nature both of
the human and the divine is falsified.

(1) The error in human things ; the confusion blurs the clear outlines of human relations by introducing into them the Perfection
that properly belongs to the non-human. It
thus creates the bastard conception of *Personality*. In literature it leads to romanticism
. . . but I deal with the nature of these errors
later.

(2) The confusion created in the absolute
values of religion and ethics is even greater.
It distorts the real nature of ethical values
by deriving them out of essentially subjective things, like human desires and feelings ;

and all attempts to " explain " religion, on a
humanist basis, whether it be Christianity,
or an alien religion like Buddhism, must
always be futile. As a minor example of
this, take the question of immortality. It
seems paradoxical at first sight, that the
Middle Ages, which lacked entirely the conception of personality, had a real belief in
immortality ; while thought since the Renaissance, which has been dominated by the
belief in personality, has not had the same
conviction. You might have expected that
it would be the people who thought they
really had something worth preserving who
would have thought they were immortal,
but the contrary is the case. Moreover,
those thinkers since the Renaissance who
have believed in immortality and who have
attempted to give explanations of it, have,
in my opinion, gone wrong, because they
have dealt with it in terms of the category of
individuality. The problem can only be pro-
fitably dealt with by being entirely re-stated.
This is just one instance of the way in which
thought about these things, in terms of categories appropriate only to human and vital
things, distorts them.

.   .   .   .   .   .

The Two Periods.—The importance of this
difference between the two conceptions of
the nature of man becomes much more
evident when it is given an historical setting.
When this somewhat abstract antithesis is

seen to be at the root of the difference between two historical periods, it begins to seem much more solid ; in this way one gives it body.

The first of these historical periods is that of the Middle Ages in Europe—from Augustine, say, to the Renaissance ; the second from the Renaissance to now. The ideology of the first period is religious ; of the second, humanist. The difference between them is fundamentally nothing but the difference between these two conceptions of man.

Everyone would assent to the statement that on the whole the first period believed in the dogma of original sin, and the second did not. But this is not enough. It is necessary to realise the immense importance of this difference in belief, to realise that in reality almost everything else springs from it. In order to understand a period it is necessary not so much to be acquainted with its more defined opinions as with the doctrines which are thought of not as doctrines, but as FACTS. (The moderns, for example, do not look for their belief in *Progress* as an opinion, but merely as a recognition of fact.) There are certain doctrines which for a particular period seem not doctrines, but inevitable categories of the human mind. Men do not look on them merely as correct opinion, for they have become so much a part of the mind, and lie so far back, that they are never really conscious of them at all. They do not see them, but other things *through* them. It is these abstract ideas at the centre, the things which they take for granted, that characterise a period. There are in each period certain doctrines, a denial of which is looked on by the men of that period just as we might look on the assertion that two and two make five. It is these abstract things at the centre, these *doctrines* felt as *facts*, which are the source of all the other more material characteristics of a period. For the Middle Ages these " facts " were the belief in the subordination of man to certain absolute values, the radical imperfection of man, the doctrine of original sin. Everyone would assent to the assertion that these beliefs were held by the men of the Middle Ages. But that is not enough. It is necessary to realise that *these beliefs were the centre of their whole civilisation, and that even the character of their economic life was regulated by them*—in particular by the kind of ethics which springs from the acceptance of sin as a fact. It is only lately that the importance of the relation has been recognised, and a good deal of interesting work has been carried out on these lines in investigating the connection between the ideology of St Thomas Aquinas and the economic life of his time.

Turn now to the second period. This does not seem to form a coherent period like the first. But it is possible to show, I think, that all thought since the Renaissance, in spite of its apparent variety, in reality forms one coherent whole. It all rests on the same presuppositions which were denied by the previous period. It all rests on the same conception of the nature of man, and all exhibits the same complete inability to realise the meaning of the dogma of Original Sin. In this period not only has its philosophy, its literature, and ethics been based on this new conception of man as fundamentally good, as sufficient, as the measure of things, but a good case can even be made out for regarding many of its characteristic economic features as springing entirely from this central abstract conception.

Not only that, but I believe that the real source of the immense change at the Renaissance should be sought not so much in some material cause, but in the gradual change of attitude about this seemingly abstract matter. Men's categories changed ; the things they took for granted changed. Everything followed from that.

There are economists now who believe that this period has been capitalist because it *desired*, it had the will, to be so. An essential preliminary to the growth of capitalism for them is, then, the growth of the capitalist " spirit." Other ages have not been industrial, not because they lacked the capacity, the scientific intelligence, but because on the whole they did not *desire* to be industrial because they lacked this particular " spirit."

We may note that Max Weber, one of the most remarkable economists of this school, sees in " the spontaneous change in religious experience (at the Renaissance), and the corresponding new ethical ideals by which life was regulated—one of the strongest roots of the capitalist spirit."

The thoroughness with which these two conceptions of man penetrate the life of their respective periods can be illustrated by the difference between their arts. What is the difference between modern art since the Renaissance, and Byzantine mosaic, which we may take as most typical of the other period ? Renaissance art we may call a " vital " art in that it depends on pleasure in the reproduction of human and natural forms. Byzantine art is the exact contrary of this. There is nothing vital in it ; the emotion you get from it is not a pleasure in the reproduction of natural or human life. The disgust with the trivial and accidental characteristics of living shapes, the searching after an austerity, a *perfection* and rigidity which vital things can never have, lead here to the use of forms which can almost be called geometrical. Man is subordinate to certain absolute values : there is no delight in the human form, leading to its *natural* reproduction ; it is always distorted to fit into the more abstract forms which convey an intense religious emotion.

These two arts thus correspond exactly

53

to the thought of their respective periods. Byzantine art to the ideology which looks on man and all existing things as imperfect and sinful in comparison with certain abstract values and *perfections*. The other art corresponds to the humanist ideology, which looks on man and life as good, and which is thus in a relation of harmony with existence. Take Goethe as typical of the period. " Human nature knows itself one with the world, and consequently feels the outer world not as something foreign to it, but recognises it as the answering counterpart to the sensations of its own inner world."

Such a humanism in all its varying forms of pantheism, rationalism and idealism, really constitutes a complete anthropomorphisation of the world, and leads naturally to art which is founded on the pleasure to be derived from vital forms.

The End of Humanism.—Now it should be noted that the coherent attitude and art of these two periods have occurred many times before in history. The Renaissance period corresponds very nearly both in its conception of man and in its art to the classical. The Byzantine art corresponds to many other geometric arts in the past, to Egyptian and Indian, for example, both, also, civilisations with a similar religious, non-humanistic conception of man. In the same way, then, it may be possible that the humanist period we live in may also come to an end, to be followed by a revival of the anti-humanist attitude. In saying this I do not in the least wish to imply any mechanical view of history as an inevitable alternation of such periods ; I am so far from such scepticism about the matter, that I regard the difference between the two attitudes as simply the difference between true and false. The great obstacle which prevents people seeing the possibility of such a change is the apparently *necessary* character of the humanist conception. But the same situation formerly existed in æsthetics. One result of the fact that both classical and modern art spring from a similar attitude to the world, is that we tend to look on these arts as *Art* itself ; the art of other periods we have regarded as archæology or ethnology. We neglected Byzantine art, for example, just as we neglected scholastic philosophy. . . . May it not, then, be significant that it is only just lately that we have begun to understand these other arts ? . . . May not the change of sensibility, in a region like æsthetics, a by-path in which we are, as it were, off our guard, be some indication that the *humanist tradition is breaking up*—for individuals here and there, at any rate ?

.   .   .   .   .   .

When I say that it may be breaking up for individuals, I ought to correct a little this picture of the two contrasted periods.

55

While such periods are on the whole coherent, they are never absolutely so. You always get people who really belong to the other period. At the beginning of a period you have the people who continue the tradition of the preceding period, and at the end those who prepare the change to that which follows. At the beginning of the Christian period you have many of the Fathers continuing the classical conception of man. At the same time as St Augustine, you get Pelagius, who has many resemblances to Rousseau, and might easily be applauded at a meeting of *progressives*. It is, as a rule, on such people that the men like Pico, who come at the end of a period, and prepare the change to the next, base themselves.

There is a similar overlapping of the religious period into the humanist one. It was this overlapping which was in reality responsible for the virtues which we often find in the earlier humanists, and which disappeared so completely when humanity attained its full development in romanticism. Compare, for example, the early Protestants and the Puritans with the sloppy thought of their descendants to-day.

Moreover, you may get, at any stage in the history of such a period, isolated individuals, whose whole attitude and ideology really belong to the opposed period. The greatest example of such an individual is, of course, Pascal. Everything that I shall say later in these notes is to be regarded merely as a prolegomena to the reading of Pascal, as an attempt to remove the difficulties of comprehension engendered in us by the humanism of our period.

When I say that I think that humanism is breaking up, and that a new period is commencing, I should like to guard against exaggeration by two reservations.

(1) I do not in the least imagine that humanism is breaking up merely to make place for a new mediævalism. The only thing the new period will have in common with mediævalism will be the subordination of man to certain absolute values. The analogy of art may again help us here. Both Byzantine and Egyptian art spring from an attitude towards life which made it impossible to use the accidental shapes of living things as symbols of the divine. Both consequently are geometrical in character ; but with this very general quality the resemblance ends. Compare a Byzantine relief of the best period with the design on a Greek vase, and an Egyptian relief. The abstract geometrical character of the Byzantine relief makes it much nearer to the Egyptian than to the Greek work ; yet a certain elegance in the line-ornament shows that it has developed out of the Greek. If the Greek had never existed it could not have the character it

has. In the same way, a new anti-humanist ideology could not be a mere revival of mediævalism. The humanist period has developed an honesty in science, and a certain conception of freedom of thought and action which will remain.

(2) I do not imagine that men themselves will change in any way. Men differ very little in every period. It is only our categories that change. Whatever we may think of sin, we shall always be sensual. Men of different sorts exist in constant proportion in different generations. But different circumstances, different prevailing ideologies, bring different types to the top. Exactly the same type existed in the Middle Ages as now. This constancy of man thus provides perhaps the greatest hope of the possibility of a radical transformation of society.

The Renaissance. — For an understanding of the way in which everything really depends on these abstract conceptions of the nature of man a study of the Renaissance is important.

The best-known work on the Renaissance, while valuable historically, seems to me to miss the whole point, for this reason : It describes the emergence of the new attitude towards life, of the new conception of man, as it might describe the gradual discovery of the conception of gravitation—that is, as the gradual emergence of something which once established would remain always, the period before being characterised thus as a *privation* of the new thing. The whole point of the thing is missed if we do not recognise that the new attitude towards man at the Renaissance was thus just an *attitude*, one attitude amongst other possible ones, deliberately chosen. It is better to describe it as a heresy, a mistaken adoption of false conceptions.

In an account of the Renaissance three things should be noticed :

(1) The changed conception itself, the putting of the Perfection into man, man no longer endowed with original sin, but by nature good. In Machiavelli you get the conception of human nature as a natural power, as living energy. Mankind is not by nature bad, but subject to passions. The absolute standards in comparison with which man was sinful disappear, and life itself is *accepted* as the measure of all values. You get Lorenzo Valla (1407) in his *De Voluptate*, daring to assert for the first time that pleasure was the highest good. A secondary consequence of this acceptance of life is the development of the conception of personality. The stages in this emphasis on the individual from Petrarch (1304) to Montaigne can be easily followed.

Michelet writes, "To the discovery of the outward world the Renaissance added a still greater achievement by bringing to light the full, the whole nature of man." This is ridiculous. The proper way to put the matter is to say that the decay into a false conception of values did in this way bring certain compensations with it.

(2) So with the establishment of the new conception of man as good, with the conception of personality comes an increased interest in the actual characteristics of man. This is at first manifested indirectly in literature. You get autobiographies for the first time—those of Cellini and Cardan, for example. It leads later, however, to more direct study of man's emotions and character, of what we should call psychology. You get works like Vives, *De Anima*, and Telesio, *De Rerum Natura*.

(3) This new study of man, this new psychology, or anthropology, has considerable influence on the philosophers who provided a conceptual clothing for the new attitude, and worked out its consequences in ethics and politics . . . on Descartes, Hobbes, and Spinoza, for example.

This process is worth while following in considerable detail for the following reason : It is necessary to emphasise how very coherent in thought such periods are, everything being in them really dependent on certain instinctive ways of judging, which, for the period, have the status of *natural* categories of the mind. The moderns, whether philosophers or reformers, make constant appeals to certain ideals, which they assume everybody will admit as natural and inevitable for the emancipated man. What these are you may discover from peroration of speeches—even from scrap books. " To thine own true self, etc. . . . Over the portal of the new world, *Be Thyself* shall be written. . . . Culture is not satisfied till we all come to a perfect man . . . the free growth of personality "—and so on. We think these things not because they are inevitable ways of thinking, but because we absorb them unconsciously from the humanist tradition which moulds the actual apparatus of our thought. They can all be traced back to the Stoics, Epicureans, and Pantheists of the Renaissance. The detailed exposition of the process by which this attitude was gradually embodied in the conceptional apparatus we inherit may do more than anything else to convince us how very far it is from being an inevitable attitude.

Partial Reactions.—It is important to distinguish two stages inside the modern period —*humanism* properly so called, and *romanticism*. The new conception of man as fundamentally good manifests itself at first in a more heroic form. In art, Donatello, Michael Angelo, or Marlowe might stand for this period. I do not deny that humanism of this kind has a certain attraction. But it deserves no admiration, for it bears in itself the seed which is bound inevitably later to develop into sentimental, utilitarian romanticism. Such humanism could have no permanence; however heroic at the start, it was bound sooner or later to end in Rousseau. There is the parallel development in art. Just as humanism leads to Rousseau so Michael Angelo leads to Greuze.

There are people who, disgusted with romanticism, wish for us to go back to the classical period, or who, like Nietzsche, wish us to admire the Renaissance. But such partial reactions will always fail, for they are only half measures—it is no good returning to humanism, for that will itself degenerate into romanticism.

This is one type of an *inadequate reaction* against humanism. There are at the present many indications of other *partial* reactions. In philosophy and ethics, for example, the work of Moore and Husserl, which is often attacked as a kind of scholasticism. A complete reaction from the subjectivism and relativism of humanist ethics should contain two elements: (1) the establishment of the *objective* character of ethical values, (2) a satisfactory ethic not only looks on values as *objective*, but establishes an order or *hierarchy* among such values, which it also regards as absolute and objective.

Now while the school of Moore and Husserl break the humanist tradition in the first matter, they seem to continue it quite uncritically in the second. In as far, then, as they free ethical values from the anthropomorphism involved in their dependence on human desires and feeling, they have created the machinery of an anti-humanist reaction which will proceed much further than they ever intended.

THE RELIGIOUS ATTITUDE

IN discussing the religious as contrasted with the humanist attitude I said above: " While it tends to find expression in myth it is independent of myth ; it is, however, much more intimately connected with dogma." I want to make this clearer by a more detailed account of what I mean by " an attitude " in this context.

The main purpose of these pages is a practical one. I want to show that certain generally held " principles " are false. But the only method of controversy in any such fundamental matter of dispute is an " abstract " one ; a method which deals with the abstract conceptions on which opinions really rest.

You think A is true ; I ask why. You reply, that it follows from B. But why is B true ? because it follows from C, and so on. You get finally to some very abstract attitude (h) which you assume to be self-evidently true. This is the central conception from which more detailed opinion about political principles, for example, proceeds. Now if your opponent reasons correctly, and you are unable to show that he has falsely deduced A from B, then you are driven to the abstract plane of (h), for it is here that the difference between you really has its root. And it is only on this abstract plane that a discussion on any fundamental divergence of opinion can usefully be carried on.

Any attempt to change (h), however, should be prefaced by some account of the nature of such abstract attitudes, and the process by which we come to adopt them.

It is possible to trace, in every man's mind, then, trains leading in various directions, from his detailed ethical and political opinions, back to a few of these central attitudes.

A......B......C............(h)

Instead, of the first concrete statement " A is true," we might have " A is good " ; in which case (h) would be an ultimate *value ;* the process, however, is the same. Another metaphor, by which we may describe the place of (h) in our thought, is to compare it to the axes, to which we refer the position of a moving point, or the framework, on which A and B are based. This is, perhaps, a better description, for the framework, inside which we live, is something *we take for granted ;* and in ordinary life we are very seldom conscious of (h). We are only led up to it by this dialectical questioning, described above.

All our " principles " are based on some unconscious " framework " of this kind. As a rule, then, we are quite unconscious of (h), we are only conscious of the detailed principles A and B, derived from it. Now while we probably acquire the opinions A and B consciously, the same is not true of (h). How do we come to hold it, then ? For we did not produce it ourselves, but derived it ready made from society. It came to be an essential part of our mind without our being conscious of it, because it was already implicit in all the more detailed opinions, A and B, society forced upon us. It was thus embedded in the actual matter of our thought, and as natural to us as the air ; in fact, it *is* the air that all these more concrete beliefs breathe. We thus have forced upon us, unconsciously, the whole apparatus of categories, in terms of which all our thinking must be done. The result of (h) having in this way the character of a category, is that it makes us see (A) not as an opinion, but as a fact. We never see (h) for we see all things *through* (h).

In this way these abstract categories, of course, *limit* our thinking ; our thought is compelled to move inside certain limits. We find, then, in people whose mental apparatus is based on (h) while ours is not, a certain obstinacy of intellect, a radical opposition, and incapacity to see things which, to us, are simple.

Now the limitation imposed on our thinking by such categories is sometimes quite legitimate. Some categories are objective. We cannot think of things outside of space and time, and it is quite right that we are subject to this limitation.

But (h) often belongs to the large class of pseudo-categories—categories which are not objective, and it is these that I wish to deal with here. They are exceedingly important, for the difference between the mentality of one great period of history and another really depends on the different pseudo-categories of this kind, which were imposed on every individual of the period, and in terms of which his thinking was consequently done. It is not difficult to find examples of this.

(1) A Brazilian Indian told a missionary that he was a red parrot. The missionary endeavoured to give some explanation of this statement. You mean, he said, that when you die you will *become* a red parrot, or that you are in some way related to this bird. The Indian rejected both these plausible attempts to explain away a perfectly simple fact, and repeated quite *coldly* that he *was* a red parrot. There would seem to be an impasse here then ; the missionary was *baffled* in the same way as the humanist is by the conception of sin. The explanation given by Lévy-Bruhl, who quotes the story, is that the Indian has *imposed* on him by his group a conception of the nature of an object,

which differs radically from ours. For him an object can be something else without at the same time ceasing to be itself. The accuracy of this explanation need not detain us. The point is that it serves as an illustration of the way in which minds dominated by *different* pseudo-categories, may have a very *different* perception of fact.

(2) Again, it has been recently argued that the only way to understand early Greek philosophy is to realise that it continued on the plane of speculation the categories, the ways of thinking, that had earlier created Greek religion . . . the conception of *Moira*, to which even the gods submitted . . . etc. The difference between the religious attitude and myth is here quite clear.

The more intimate connection with dogmas I referred to depends on the fact that dogma is often a fairly intellectual way of expressing these fundamental categories—the dogma of Original Sin, for example. At the Renaissance, in spite of opinion to the contrary, the philosophy did *not* express the categories, the ways of thinking which had earlier been expressed in the Christian religion ; it reversed them.

It is these categories, these abstract conceptions, which all the individuals of a period have in common, which really serve best to characterise the period. For most of the characteristics of such a period, not only in thought, but in ethics, and through ethics in

68

economics, really depend on these central abstract attitudes. But while people will readily acknowledge that this is true of the Greeks, or of Brazilian Indians, they have considerable difficulty in realising that it is also true of the modern humanist period from the Renaissance to now. The way in which we instinctively judge things we take to be the inevitable way of judging things. The pseudo-categories of the humanist attitude are thought to be on the same footing as the objective categories of space and time. It is thought to be impossible for an emancipated man to think sincerely in the categories of the religious attitude.

The reason for this is to be found in the fact already noticed that we are, as a rule, unconscious of the very abstract conceptions which underlie our more concrete opinions. What Ferrier says of real categories, " Categories may be operative when their existence is not consciously recognised. First principles of every kind have their influence, and, indeed, operate largely and profoundly long before they come to the surface of human thought, and are articulately expounded," is true also of these pseudo-categories. We are only conscious of A, B . . . and very seldom of (h). We do not see that, but other things *through it ;* and, consequently, take what we see for facts, and not for what they are— opinions based on a particular abstract valuation. This is certainly true of the *progressive*

69

ideology founded on the conception of man as fundamentally good.

It is this unconsciousness of these central abstract conceptions, leading us to suppose that the judgments of value founded on them are *natural* and *inevitable*, which makes it so difficult for anyone in the humanist tradition to look at the religious attitude as anything but a sentimental survival.

But I want to emphasise as clearly as I can, that I attach very little value indeed to the *sentiments* attaching to the religious attitude. I hold, quite coldly and intellectually as it were, that the way of thinking about the world and man, the conception of sin, and the categories which ultimately make up the religious attitude, are the *true* categories and the *right* way of thinking.

I might incidentally note here, that the way in which I have explained the action of the central abstract attitudes and ways of thinking, and the use of the word *pseudo*-categories, might suggest that I hold relativist views about their validity. But I don't. I hold the religious conception of ultimate values to be right, the humanist wrong. From the nature of things, these categories are not inevitable, like the categories of time and space, but are *equally objective*. In speaking of religion, it is to this level of abstraction that I wish to refer. I have none of the feelings of *nostalgia*, the reverence for tradition, the desire to recapture the sentiment of

Fra Angelico, which seems to animate most modern defenders of religion. All that seems to me to be bosh. What is important, is what nobody seems to realise—the dogmas like that of Original Sin, which are the closest expression of the categories of the religious attitude. That man is in no sense perfect, but a wretched creature, who can yet apprehend perfection. It is not, then, that I put up with the dogma for the sake of the sentiment, but that I may possibly swallow the sentiment for the sake of the dogma. Very few since the Renaissance have really understood the dogma, certainly very few inside the Churches of recent years. If they appear occasionally even fanatical about the very word of the dogma, that is only a secondary result of belief really grounded on sentiment. Certainly no humanist could understand the dogma. They all chatter about matters which are in comparison with this, quite secondary notions —God, Freedom, and Immortality.

The important thing is that this attitude is not merely a *contrasted* attitude, which I am interested in, as it were, for purpose of *symmetry* in historical exposition, but a real attitude, perfectly possible for us to-day. To see this is a kind of conversion. It radically alters our physical perception ; so that the world takes on an entirely different aspect.

71

MODERN ART AND
ITS PHILOSOPHY

*The fright of the mind before the
unknown created not only the
first gods, but also the first art.*

MODERN ART AND ITS PHILOSOPHY 1914.

I

My title is perhaps misleading, in that it lays emphasis on modern art * itself, rather than on its philosophy. Only the last half of what I am going to say deals with the art itself ; the first part is devoted to entirely general considerations, which seem to me to be necessary to its proper understanding. I know that this may appear an unnecessary and rather fantastic superstructure. An artist might feel that I was merely bringing in all kinds of vague literary considerations, which have very little to do with the art itself. New movements in art are generally accompanied by muddle-headed but enthusiastic attempts to connect them with quite unconnected movements in philosophy, which appear to the journalist's mind to be coloured by the same quality of excitement. There are people, for example, who try to connect cubism with Plato. The artist, recognising these interpretations as the mere confused

* [The author refers to the new movements which were beginning to attract attention at the date of this paper which was prepared for a lecture delivered before the Quest Society on January 22, 1914.—H. R.]

sentimentality that they are, may yet accept them good-humouredly, in as far as they lend some kind of support to a new movement.

But it seems to me that there is another way of dealing with an art from a general point of view which follows the contours of the thing itself a little more closely. It may be justified in that it attempts to deal, not so much with the art itself, as with the language in which the artist or critic attempts to explain that art. The critic in explaining a new direction often falsifies it by his use of a vocabulary derived from the old position. The thought or vocabulary of one's period is an extraordinarily difficult thing to break away from. While an artist may have emancipated himself from his own period as far as his art is concerned, while a spectator may have emancipated himself by looking at the art of other periods in museums, yet the mental, or more accurately speaking, the linguistic emancipations of the two, may not have gone forward parallel with the artistic one.

Quite definitely what I mean is this : I think that the new art differs not in degree, but in kind, from the art we are accustomed to, and that there is a danger that the understanding of the new may be hindered by a way of looking on art which is only appropriate to the art that has preceded it. The general considerations I put forward are of this kind. This new art is geometrical in character,

while the art we are accustomed to is vital *
and organic. It so happens that there have
been many other geometric arts in the past.
I think that a consideration of these arts may
help one to understand what is coming, and
to avoid the falsification I have spoken of.
I may also by this method be enabled to
remove certain prejudices which stand in the
way of appreciation of this art.

My remarks are likely to appear confused,
as my argument, such as it is, is composed of
three or four parts, only one of which I have
space enough to develop in detail. I can perhaps give them more shape, by laying down to
begin with certain theses which I assert to be
true, but do not attempt to prove here :—

(1) There are two kinds of art, geometrical and vital, absolutely distinct in
kind from one another. These two arts
are not modifications of one and the
same art but pursue different aims and
are created for the satisfaction of different
necessities of the mind.

* I might add a note here on my use of the word vital. This
word instead of having the specific meaning it should have, has
come to have the meaning of living in the sense of strong and
creative as opposed to weak and imitative. In fact the difference between vital and non-vital has simply come to be the
difference between good and bad. It need perhaps hardly be
pointed out that my use of the word vital in this lecture has
nothing whatever to do with this sense of the word. Vital and
mechanical or geometrical arts may both be vital or non-vital in
the current use of the word. A man might conceivably say that
the geometrical Byzantine art displayed a certain lack of vitality
in this sense. I might dispute that; but even if I did not I
think that my use of the word vital, defined as I have defined it,
is permissible.

77

(2) Each of these arts springs from and corresponds to a certain general attitude towards the world. You get long periods of time in which only one of these arts with its corresponding mental attitudes prevails. The vital art of Greece and the Renaissance corresponded to a certain attitude of mind and the geometrical has always gone with a different general attitude, of greater intensity than this.

And (3)—this is really the point I am making for—that the re-emergence of geometrical art may be the precursor of the re-emergence of the corresponding attitude towards the world, and so, of the break up of the Renaissance humanistic attitude. The fact that this change comes first in art, before it comes in thought, is easily understandable for this reason. So thoroughly are we soaked in the spirit of the period we live in, so strong is its influence over us, that we can only escape from it in an unexpected way, as it were, a side direction like art.

I am emphasising then, the absolute character of the difference between these two arts, not only because it is important for the understanding of the new art itself, but because it enables me to maintain much wider theses.

That is the logical order in which I present my convictions. I did not naturally arrive

at them in that order. I came to believe
first of all, for reasons quite unconnected
with art, that the Renaissance attitude was
coming to an end, and was then confirmed
in that by the emergence of this art. I com-
menced by a change in philosophy and illus- | *phil then art*
trated this by a change in art rather than
vice versa. A thesis like my last one is so
sweeping that it sounds a little empty. It
would be quite ludicrous for me to attempt
to state such a position in the space of the
half page I intend to devote to it, but perhaps
I can make it sound more plausible by saying
how I came personally to believe it. You
will have to excuse my putting it in auto-
biographical shape, for, after all, the break-up
of a general attitude if it ever occurs will be a
collection of autobiographies. First of all
comes the conviction that in spite of its
apparent extraordinary variety, European
philosophy since the Renaissance does form
a unity. You can separate philosophy into
two parts, the technical and scientific part,
that which more properly would be called
metaphysics, and another part in which the
machinery elaborated in the first is used to
express the philosopher's attitude towards
the world, what may be called his conclusions.
These emerge in the last chapter of the book.
In the first chapters the philosopher may be
compared to a man in armour ; he intimidates
you, as a kind of impersonal machine. In the
last chapter you perceive him naked, as per-

79

fectly human. Every philosopher says the
world is other than it seems to be ; in the last
chapter he tells you what he thinks it is.
As he has taken the trouble to prove it, you
may assume that he regards the final picture
of the world he gives as satisfactory.

Now here is my point. In a certain sense,
all philosophy since the Renaissance is satisfied with a certain conception of the relation
of man to the world. Now what is this conception ? You get the first hint of it in the
beginnings of the Renaissance itself, in a
person like Pico Della Mirandola, for example.
You get the hint of an idea there of something,
which finally culminates in a doctrine which
is the opposite of the doctrine of original
sin : the belief that man as a part of nature
was after all something satisfactory. The
change which Copernicus is supposed to have
brought about is the exact contrary of the
fact. Before Copernicus, man was not the
centre of the world ; after Copernicus he
was. You get a change from a certain profundity and intensity to that flat and insipid
optimism which, passing through its first
stage of decay in Rousseau, has finally cul-
minated in the state of slush in which we have
the misfortune to live. If you want a proof
of the radical difference between these two
attitudes, you have only to look at the
books which are written now on Indian
religion and philosophy. There is a sheer
anæmic inability to understand the stark

uncompromising bleakness of this religious attitude.

It may seem paradoxical in view of the extraordinary emphasis laid on life by philosophy at the present day, to assert that this Renaissance attitude is coming to an end. But I think that this efflorescence is its last effort.

About the time that I arrived at this kind of conviction I saw Byzantine mosaics for the first time. This led me a step further towards the conviction I have expressed in this thesis. I had got myself away from the contemporary view, and (as I shall illustrate later in the case of art, the first attempt to formulate a different attitude being always a return to archaism) I was inclined to hold a view not very different from that of that period. At that time, then, I was impressed by these mosaics, not as by something exotic, but as expressing quite directly an attitude I agreed with. Owing to this accident, I was able to see a geometrical art, as it were from the inside. I then saw how essential and necessary a geometrical character is in endeavouring to express a certain intensity.

Finally I recognised this geometrical character re-emerging in modern art. I am thinking particularly of certain pieces of sculpture I saw some years ago, of Mr Epstein's.

I had here then, very crudely, all the elements of the position that I put before in my three theses. At that time, in an essay by Paul Ernst on Byzantine art, I came across a reference to the work of Riegl and Worringer. In the latter particularly I found an extraordinarily clear statement, founded on an extensive knowledge of the history of art, of a view very like the one I had tried to formulate. This last year I heard him lecture and had some conversation with him at the Berlin Congress of Æsthetics. What follows is practically an abstract of Worringer's views.

II

You have these two different kinds of art. You have first the art which is natural to you, Greek art and modern art since the Renaissance. In these arts the lines are soft and vital. You have other arts like Egyptian, Indian and Byzantine, where everything tends to be angular, where curves tend to be hard and geometrical, where the representation of the human body, for example, is often entirely non-vital, and distorted to fit into stiff lines and cubical shapes of various kinds.

What is the cause of the extraordinary difference between these geometrical arts and the arts we are accustomed to admire? Why do they show none of the qualities which we are accustomed to find in art?

We may at once put on one side the idea that the difference between archaic and later art is due to a difference of capacity, the idea

82

that geometrical shapes are used because the artist had not the technical ability necessary for carving the more natural representation of the body. The characteristics of archaic art are not due to incapacity. In Egypt, at the time when the monumental sculpture showed a stylification as great as any we find in archaic art, the domestic art of the period exhibited a most astonishing realism. In pure technical ability in mastery of raw material, the Egyptians have never been surpassed. It is quite obvious that what they did was intentional.

We are forced back on the idea, then, that geometrical art differs from our own because the creators of that art had in view an object entirely different from that of the creators of more naturalistic art. The idea that an art is a satisfaction of some specific mental need, and so, that in looking at a work of art of this type it is necessary not only to think of the object itself, but of the desire it is intended to satisfy, is one which it is very difficult for us to realise for the following reason. The subjective side of an art is never forced on our notice, because it so happens that the arts with which we are familiar, the classical and our own, have the same subjective element. It never occurs to us therefore that classical art is the satisfaction of one among other possible desires, since we always think that this art is the satisfaction of *the* desire which must inevitably be behind all art. We thus erect the classical and our own conception of art into an absolute and look on all art before the classical as imperfect strivings towards it, and all after as decadence from it.

It is necessary to realise that all art is created to satisfy a particular desire—that when this desire is satisfied, you call the work beautiful; but that if the work is intended to satisfy a desire and mental need different from your own, it will necessarily appear to you to be grotesque and meaningless. We naturally do not call these geometrical arts beautiful because beauty for us is the satisfaction of a certain need, and that need is one which archaic art never set out to satisfy. What from our standpoint appears as the greatest distortion must have been, for the people who produced it, the highest beauty and the fulfilment of some desire.

Consider the difference between these two kinds, then, from this point of view.

Take first the art which is most natural to us. What tendency is behind this, what need is it designed to satisfy?

This art as contrasted with geometrical art can be broadly described as naturalism or realism—using these words in their widest sense and entirely excluding the mere imitation of nature. The source of the pleasure felt by the spectator before the products of art of this kind is a feeling of increased vitality, a process which German writers on æsthetics call empathy (Einfühlung). This process is perhaps a little too complicated for me to describe it shortly here, but putting the matter in general terms, we can say that any work of art we find beautiful is an objectification of our own pleasure in activity, and our own vitality. The worth of a line or form consists in the value of the life which it contains for us. Putting the matter more simply we may say that in this art there is always a feeling of liking for, and pleasure in, the forms and movements to be found in nature. It is obvious therefore that this art can only occur in a people whose relation to outside nature is such that it admits of this feeling of pleasure in its contemplation.

Turn now to geometrical art. It most obviously exhibits no delight in nature and no striving after vitality. Its forms are always what can be described as stiff and lifeless. The dead form of a pyramid and the suppression of life in a Byzantine mosaic show that behind these arts there must have been an impulse, the direct opposite of that which finds satisfaction in the naturalism of Greek and Renaissance art.

This is what Worringer calls the *tendency to abstraction*.

What is the nature of this tendency? What is the condition of mind of the people whose art is governed by it?

It can be described most generally as a feeling of separation in the face of outside nature.

85

SPECULATIONS

While a naturalistic art is the result of a happy pantheistic relation between man and the outside world, the tendency to abstraction, on the contrary, occurs in races whose attitude to the outside world is the exact contrary of this. This feeling of separation naturally takes different forms at different levels of culture.

Take first, the case of more primitive people. They live in a world whose lack of order and seeming arbitrariness must inspire them with a certain fear. One may perhaps get a better description of what must be their state of mind by comparing it to the fear which makes certain people unable to cross open spaces. The fear I mean here is mental, however, not physical. They are dominated by what Worringer calls a kind of spiritual " space-shyness " in face of the varied confusion and arbitrariness of existence. In art this state of mind results in a desire to create a certain abstract geometrical shape, which, being durable and permanent shall be a refuge from the flux and impermanence of outside nature. The need which art satisfies here, is not the delight in the forms of nature, which is a characteristic of all vital arts, but the exact contrary. In the reproduction of natural objects there is an attempt to purify them of their characteristically living qualities in order to make them necessary and immovable. The changing is translated into something fixed and necessary. This leads

lines

to rigid lines and dead crystalline forms, for pure geometrical regularity gives a certain pleasure to men troubled by the obscurity of outside appearance. The geometrical line is something absolutely distinct from the messiness, the confusion, and the accidental details of existing things.

It must be pointed out that this condition of fear is in no sense a necessary presupposition of the tendency to abstraction. The necessary presupposition is the idea of disharmony or separation between man and nature. In peoples like the Indian or the Byzantine this feeling of separation takes quite another form.

To sum up this view of art then : it cannot be understood by itself, but must be taken as one element in a general process of adjustment between man and the outside world. The character of that relation determines the character of the art. If there is a difference of " potential " between man and the outside world, if they are at different levels, so that the relation between them is, as it were, a steep inclined plane, then the adjustment between them in art takes the form of a tendency to abstraction. If on the contrary there is no disharmony between man and the outside world, if they are both on the same level, on which man feels himself one with nature and not separate from it, then you get a naturalistic art.

The art of a people, then, will run parallel

to its philosophy and general world outlook.
It is a register of the nature of the opposition
between man and the world. Each race is in
consequence of its situation and character
inclined to one of these two tendencies, and its
art would give you a key to its psychology.

It is easy to trace these parallel changes. I
have spoken of that feeling of space-shyness
which produced the tendency to abstraction
in primitive art. This tendency would have
been impossible in the case of a people like
the Greeks at the time when they had finally
got free from the oriental elements of their
origins and had not fallen afresh to oriental
tendencies. In such a people you get a
feeling of confidence in face of the world which
expresses itself in religion in a certain anthropomorphism. The feeling of disharmony with
the world had been destroyed by certain
favourable conditions and by increased knowledge (Rationalism). You can speak here,
then, of a classical religious period as you speak
of a classical art period. Both are only
different manifestations of the same classical
conception which Goethe defined as that in
which man " feels himself one with nature
and consequently looks upon the outside
world not as something strange, but as something which he recognises as answering to his
own feelings."

In the case of the orientals the feeling of
separation from the world could not be dis-
pelled by knowledge. Their sense of the

unfathomable existence was greater than that of the Greeks. A satisfaction with appearances is limited to Europe. It is only there that the superhuman abstract idea of the divine has been expressed by banal representation. No knowledge could damp down the Indian inborn fear of the world, since it stands, not as in the case of primitive man before knowledge, but above it. Their art consequently remained geometrical.

It is in the light of this tendency to abstraction that I wish to deal with modern art. Before doing that, however, I want to make the tendency clearer by giving some concrete examples of its working in sculpture.

In the endeavour to get away from the flux of existence, there is an endeavour to create in contrast, an absolutely enclosed material individuality. Abstraction is more difficult in the round than in the flat. With three dimensions we get the relativism and obscurity of appearance. A piece of sculpture in the round seems quite as lost in its context as does the natural object itself. There is consequently stronger stylification used in the round than is necessary in the relief. In archaic Greek sculpture, for example, the arms are bound close to the body, any division of the surface is as far as possible avoided and unavoidable divisions and articulations are given in no detail. The first gods were always pure abstractions without any resemblance to life. Any weakening of these abstract forms and approximation to reality would have let in change and life and so would have done what it was desired to avoid —it would have taken the thing out of eternity and put it into time. In monumental art, the abstract and inorganic is always used to make the organic seem durable and eternal. The first rule of monumental art must be a strong inclosure of cubical forms. It is ridiculous to suppose that the masons who carved the face of an archaic figure did not possess the capacity to separate the arms or legs from the body. The fact that they did so later in classical Greek art was not due to a progress in technical ability. The Greeks left behind the intensity of these cubical forms and replaced the abstract by the organic simply because, as their attitude to the world changed, they had different intentions. Having attained a kind of optimistic rationalism they no longer felt any desire for abstraction. They did not create gods like these earlier ones because they no longer possessed any religious intensity.

When we turn to Egyptian art, we find that in the endeavour to escape from anything that might suggest the relative and impermanent there is always the same tendency to make all the surfaces as flat as possible. In the sitting figures the legs and the body form a cubical mass out of which only the shoulders and head appear as necessary individualisation. The treatment of drapery and hair is only another example of this desire to make what is most obviously flexible and impermanent look fixed.

III

I COME now to the application of the distinction thus elaborately constructed between geometrical and vital art to what is going on at the present moment.

If the argument I have followed is correct, I stand committed to two statements :—

(1) . . . that a new geometrical art is emerging which may be considered as different in kind from the art which preceded it, it being much more akin to the geometrical arts of the past, and

(2) . . . that this change from a vital to a geometrical art is the product of and will be accompanied by a certain change of sensibility, a certain change of general attitude, and that this new attitude will differ in kind from the humanism which has prevailed from the Renaissance to now, and will have certain analogies to the attitude of which geometrical art was the expression in the past.

Naturally both of these sweeping statements run a good deal ahead of the facts and of my ability to prove them. I must here, therefore, make the same qualification and warning about both of the statements. Though both the new Weltanschauung and the new geometrical art will have certain analogies with corresponding periods in the past, yet it is not for a moment to be supposed that there is anything more than an analogy here. The new geometrical art will probably in the end not in the least resemble archaic art, nor will the new attitude to the world be very much like the Byzantine, for example. As to what actually they both will culminate in, it would obviously be ludicrous for me to attempt to say. It would be more ludicrous to attempt to do this in the case of the general attitude, than it would in the case of the art itself. For one of my points at the beginning of this paper was that one's mind is so soaked in the thought and language of the period, that one can only perceive the break-up of that period in a region like <u>art</u> which is—when one's mind is focussed on thought itself—<u>a kind of side activity.</u>

One can only make certain guesses at the new attitude by the use of analogy. Take two other attitudes of the past which went with geometrical art : say primitive and Byzantine. There is a certain likeness and a certain unlikeness in relation to man and the outside world. The primitive springs from what we have called a kind of mental space-shyness, which is really an attitude of fear before the world ; the <u>Byzantine from what may be called, inaccurately, a kind of contempt for the world.</u> Though these two attitudes differ very much, yet there is a <u>common element in the idea of separation</u> as opposed to the more

92

intimate feeling towards the world in classical
and renaissance thought.   In comparison with
the flat and insipid optimism of the belief in
progress, the new attitude may be in a certain   *contr Futurism*
sense inhuman, pessimistic.   Yet its pessim-
ism will not be world-rejecting in the sense in
which the Byzantine was.

But one is on much surer ground in dealing   *basis of*
with the art itself.   On what grounds does one   *idea of*
base this belief that a new geometrical art is   *change in*
appearing ?   There is first the more negative   *art*
proof provided by a change of taste.

You get an extraordinary interest in similar
arts in the past, in Indian sculpture, in Byzantine art, in archaic art generally, and this
interest is not as before a merely archæo-
logical one.   The things are liked directly,
almost as they were liked by the people who
made them, as being direct expressions of an
attitude which you want to find expressed.
I do not think for a moment that this is conscious.   I think that under the influence of a
false conception of the nature of art, that
most people, even when they feel it, falsify
their real appreciation by the vocabulary they
use—naïve, fresh, charm of the exotic, and
so on.

A second and more positive proof is to be
found in the actual creation of a new modern
geometrical art.

You get at the present moment in Europe   *Art*
a most extraordinary confusion in art, a
complete breaking away from tradition.   So

93

confusing is it that most people lump it altogether as one movement and are unaware
that it is in fact composed of a great many
distinct and even contradictory elements,
being a complex movement of parts that are
merely reactionary, parts that are dead, and
with one part only containing the possibility
of development. When I speak of a new
complex geometrical art then, I am not
thinking of the whole movement. I am speaking of one element which seems to be gradually
hardening out, and separating itself from the
others. I don't want anyone to suppose, for
example, that I am speaking of futurism
which is, in its logical form, the exact opposite
of the art I am describing, being the deification
of the flux, the last efflorescence of impressionism. I also exclude a great many things
which—as I shall attempt to show later were
perhaps necessary preliminaries to this art,
but which have now been passed by—most
of the work in fact which is included under the
term post-impressionism—Gauguin, Maillol,
Brancusi.

If space allowed I could explain why I
also exclude certain elements of cubism,
what I might call analytical cubism—the
theories about interpenetration which you
get in Metzinger for example.

IV

BEFORE dealing actually with this work I ought to qualify what I have said a little. I have put the matter in a rather too ponderous way by talking about the new general attitude. That is perhaps dealing with the matter on the wrong plane. It would have been quite possible for this change to come about without the artists themselves being conscious of this change of general attitude towards the world at all. When I say " conscious " I mean conscious in this formulated and literary fashion. The change of attitude would have taken place, but it might only have manifested itself in a certain change of sensibility in the artist, and in so far as he expresses himself in words, in a certain change of vocabulary. The change of attitude betrays itself by changes in the epithets that a man uses, perhaps disjointedly, to express his admiration for the work he admires. Most of us cannot state our position, and we use adjectives which in themselves do not explain what we mean, but which, for a group for a certain time, by a kind of tacit convention become the " porters " or " bearers " of the complex new attitude which we all recognise that we have in company, but which we cannot describe or analyse. At the present time you get this change shown in the value given to certain adjectives. Instead of epithets

Lewis Pound

like graceful, beautiful, etc., you get epithets
like austere, mechanical, clear cut, and bare,
used to express admiration.

Putting on one side all this talk of a " new
attitude " of which the artist in some cases
may not be conscious at all, what is the nature
of the new sensibility which betrays itself
in this change of epithets ? Putting it at its
lowest terms, namely that a man was unconscious of any change of aim, but only felt
that he preferred certain shapes, certain forms,
etc., and that his work was moulded by that
change of sensibility, what is the nature of
that change of sensibility at the present
moment ? Expressed generally, there seems
to be a desire for austerity and bareness, a
striving towards structure and away from the
messiness and confusion of nature and natural
things. Take a concrete matter like the
use of line and surface. In all art since the
Renaissance, the lines used are what may be
called vital lines. In any curve there is a
certain empirical variation which makes the
curve not mechanical. The lines are obviously
drawn by a hand and not by a machine.
You get Ruskin saying that no artist could
draw a straight line. As far as sensibility
goes you get a kind of shrinking from anything that has the appearance of being mechanical. An artist, suppose, has to draw a
part of a piece of machinery, where a certain
curve is produced by the intersection of a
plane and a cylinder. It lies in the purpose

96

of the engine and it is obviously the intention
of the engineer that the line shall be a perfect
and mechanical curve. The artists in drawing the two surfaces and their intersection
would shrink from reproducing this mechanical
accuracy, would instinctively pick out all the
accidental scratches which make the curve
empirical and destroy its geometrical and
mechanical character. In the new art on
the contrary there is no shrinking of that kind
whatever. There is rather a desire to avoid
those lines and surfaces which look pleasing
and organic, and to use lines which are clean,
clear-cut and mechanical. You will find
artists expressing admiration for engineer's
drawings, where the lines are clean, the curves
all geometrical, and the colour, laid on to
show the shape of a cylinder for example,
gradated absolutely mechanically. You will
find a sculptor disliking the pleasing kind of
patina that comes in time on an old bronze
and expressing admiration for the hard clean
surface of a piston rod. If we take this to
be in fact the new sensibility, and regard it as
the culmination of the process of breaking-up
and transformation in art, that has been
proceeding since the impressionists, it seems
to me that the history of the last twenty
years becomes more intelligible. It suddenly
enables one to look at the matter in a new light.

Put the matter in an a priori way. Admitting the premiss that a new direction is
gradually defining itself, what would you

expect to happen ? As a help to this reconstruction, recall what was said about the relation between the various geometrical arts of the past at the beginning of the last part of my paper, to the effect that there are always certain common elements, but also that each period has its own specific qualities. This new art, towards which things were working, was bound, then, to have certain elements in common with past geometric archaic arts, but at the same time as an art springing up to-day, it would necessarily exhibit certain original and peculiar qualities due to that fact. Consider then the beginning of the movement. No man at the beginning of a movement of this kind can have any clear conception of its final culmination — that would be to anticipate the result of a process of creation. Of which of the two elements of the new geometric art—that which it has in common with similar arts in the past, or that which is specific and peculiar to it—is an artist most likely to be conscious at the beginning of a movement ? Most obviously of those elements which are also to be found in the past. Here then you get the explanation of the fact which may have puzzled some people, that a new and modern art, something which was to culminate in a use of structural organisation akin to machinery, should have begun by what seemed like a romantic return to barbarous and primitive art, apparently inspired by a kind of nostalgia for the past.

Another cause reinforcing the tendency to
the archaic is the difficulty of at once finding
an appropriate method of expression. Though
the artist feels that he must have done with
the contemporary means of expression, yet a
new and more fitting method is not easily
created. The way from intention to expression does not come naturally, as it were from
in outwards. A man has first to obtain a
foothold in this, so to speak, alien and external
world of material expression, at a point near
the one he is making for. He has to utilise
some already existing methods of expression
and work from them to the one that expresses
his own personal conception more accurately
and naturally. What happened then was
this—a certain change of direction took place,
beginning negatively with a feeling of dissatisfaction with, and reaction against, existing art. You get a breaking away from
contemporary methods of expression, a new
direction, an intenser perception of things
striving towards expression, and as this intensity was fundamentally the same kind of
intensity as that expressed in certain archaic
arts, it quite naturally and legitimately found
a foothold in these archaic yet permanent
formulæ. A certain archaicism then, just as
it is at the beginning helpful to an artist
though he may afterwards repudiate it, is an
almost necessary stage in the preparation of a
new movement.

This seems to me to be the best way of

describing and understanding the movement that has had the label of Post-impressionism affixed to it in England. Though perhaps the individual artists of that time would never have gone further than they did, yet looking at them from this general point of view, it is best to regard them as the preliminary and temporary stage of experimentation in the preparation of a suitable method of expression for a new and intenser sensibility. It is not necessary to do more than mention an obvious example such as Gauguin.

The case of Cézanne is more important for it is out of him that the second stage of the movement that I have called analytical Cubism has developed. It is also interesting since it is only lately that it has been recognised how fundamentally Cézanne differed from his contemporaries, the impressionists. It was against their fluidity that he reacted. He wanted, so he said, to make of impressionism something solid and durable like old art.

Before commenting on this, I must recall again the distinction I have used between naturalism and abstraction. I want to point out that even in a period of natural and vital art a certain shadow of the tendency to abstraction still remains in the shape of formal composition. Some kinds of composition are attempts to make the organic look rigid and durable. In most landscapes, of course, the composition is rhythmical and not formal in this extreme sense, and so it is not an expression of a tendency to abstraction. With this in mind, look at one of Cézanne's latest n.b pictures, " Women Bathing," where all the lines are ranged in a pyramidal shape, and the women are distorted to fit this shape. You will, if you are accustomed to look for pleasing rhythmical composition in a picture, be repelled rather than attracted by this pyramidal composition. The form is so strongly accentuated, so geometric in character, that it almost lifts the painting out of the sphere of " vital " art into that of abstract art. It is much more akin to the composition you find in the Byzantine mosaic (of the empress Theodora) in Ravenna, than it is to anything which can be found in the art of the Renaissance.

If you deny the existence of a " tendency to abstraction " at all in art, you will naturally deny the apparent appearance of it in Cézanne. You will say that the simplifications of planes (out of which of course cubism grew), is not due to any " tendency towards abstraction," but is the result of an effort to give a more solid kind of reality in the object. You will assert that when Cézanne said that the forms of nature could be reduced to the cone, the cylinder, and the sphere, that he meant something quite different from the obvious meaning of his words. This misconception of Cézanne results from the fact that you have refused to see the obvious truth, that there is

in him a hint of that " tendency to abstraction " that is found in certain arts of the past.
The difference between the use of planes in
Cézanne and in the cubists themselves, is
not that between a simplification based on
observation of nature and a mere playing
about with formulæ. Both simplifications are
based on the research into nature, but their
value to the artist does not lie in their origin,
but in the use that is made of them.

That is, I think, how one ought to look on
these painters, quite apart from the qualities
they show as painters belonging to the past
vital period of painting. They are interesting
to us as showing the first gradual emergence
in a state of experimentation, of this new
geometrical art which will be created by a
tendency to abstraction. I should, properly
speaking, now attempt to define the characteristics of the new art as they emerge
from this experimental stage, but that is
difficult for me to do as the thing itself is
still to a large extent experimental. I cannot say what artists will make of this method ;
the construction of this is their business,
not mine. That is the fun of the thing. I
await myself the development of that art
with the greatest impatience. My feeling
about the matter is this. I look at most
cubist pictures with a certain feeling of de-
pression. They are from a certain point of
view, confused. If I may be allowed to go
against my own principles for a minute, and

to describe abstract things in a metaphor borrowed from organic life, I should say they look rather like embryos. I think they will soon open out and grow distinct. I picture what is about to happen in this way. A man whose form is, as it were, dimly discerned in hay, stands up, shakes the hay off him, and proceeds to walk, *i.e.* he proceeds to do something. Dropping the metaphor then, cubism ceases to be analytical, and is transformed into a constructive geometrical art. The elements and the method patiently worked out by analysis begin to be used. If you want a concrete example of the difference I mean, compare the work illustrated in Metzinger's book on cubism, with that of Mr Epstein and Mr Lewis. This difference seems to me to be important for this reason. There are many who, when the matter has been explained to them, can understand what the early cubists are trying to do. They follow the sort of analysis they have made, but they cannot for the life of them see how it can go on, or how it can develop into a new art. And I believe that this is in reality the source of the baffled feeling of most people when confronted by such art.

V

IN conclusion, I might hazard some con-
jectures as to the probable nature of the
specific and peculiar quality which will differentiate this new geometrical art from its
predecessors. As far as one can see, the new
" tendency towards abstraction " will culminate, not so much in the simple geometrical
forms found in archaic art, but in the more
complicated ones associated in our minds with
the idea of machinery. In this association
with machinery will probably be found the
specific differentiating quality of the new
art. It is difficult to define properly at the
present moment what this relation to machinery will be. It has nothing whatever to do
with the superficial notion that one must
beautify machinery. It is not a question of
dealing with machinery in the spirit, and with
the methods of existing art, but of the creation
of a new art having an organisation, and
governed by principles, which are at present
exemplified unintentionally, as it were, in
machinery. It is hardly necessary to repeat
at this stage of the argument, that it will not
aim at the satisfaction of that particular
mental need, which in a vital art results in the
production of what is called beauty. It is
aiming at the satisfaction of a different mental
need altogether. When Mr Roger Fry, there-

fore, talks as he did lately, of " machinery being as beautiful as a rose " he demonstrates what is already obvious from his work, that he has no conception whatever of this new art, and is in fact a mere verbose sentimentalist.

This association of art and machinery suggests all kinds of problems. What will be the relation to the artist and the engineer ? At present the artist is merely receptive in regard to machinery. He passively admires, for example, the superb steel structures which form the skeletons of modern buildings, and whose gradual envelopment in a parasitic covering of stone is one of the daily tragedies to be witnessed in London streets. Will the artist always remain passive, or will he take a more active part ? The working out of the relation between art and machinery can be observed at present in many curious ways. Besides the interest in machinery itself, you get the attempt to create in art, structures whose organisation, such as it is, is very like that of machinery. Most of Picasso's paintings, for instance, whatever they may be labelled, are at bottom studies of a special kind of machinery.

But here an apparently quite legitimate objection might be raised. The desire to create something mechanical in this sense might be admitted as understandable, but the question would still be asked, " Why make use of the human body in this art, *hers*

why make that look like a machine ? "
Those who are accustomed to a vital art,
the basis of whose appreciation of art is what
I have called empathy, and who consequently
derive pleasure from the reproduction of the
actual details of life, are repulsed by an art
in which something which is intended to be
a body, leaves out all these details and
qualities they expect.

Take for example one of Mr Wyndham
Lewis's pictures. It is obvious that the
artist's only interest in the human body was
in a few abstract mechanical relations perceived in it, the arm as a lever and so on. The
interest in living flesh as such, in all that
detail that makes it vital, which is pleasing,
and which we like to see reproduced, is entirely
absent.

use of organic in machine art -

But if the division that I have insisted on
in this paper—the division between the two
different tendencies producing two different
kinds of art—is valid, then this objection
falls to the ground. What you get in Mr
Lewis's pictures is what you always get inside any geometrical art. All art of this
character turns the organic into something
not organic, it tries to translate the changing
and limited, into something unlimited and
necessary. The matter is quite simple. However strong the desire for abstraction, it cannot be satisfied with the reproduction of
merely inorganic forms. A perfect cube looks
stable in comparison with the flux of appear-

ance, but one might be pardoned if one felt no particular interest in the eternity of a cube ; but if you can put man into some geometrical shape which lifts him out of the transience of the organic, then the matter is different. In pursuing such an aim you inevitably, of course, sacrifice the pleasure that comes from reproduction of the natural.

Another good example to take, would be Mr Epstein's latest work, the drawings for sculpture in the first room of his exhibition. The subjects of all of them are connected with birth. They are objected to because they are treated in what the critics are pleased to term a cubistic manner. But this seems to me a most interesting example of what I have just been talking about. The tendency to abstraction, the desire to turn the organic into something hard and durable, is here at work, not on something simple, such as you get in the more archaic work, but on something much more complicated. It is, however, the same tendency at work in both. Abstraction is much greater in the second case, because generation, which is the very essence of all the qualities which we have here called organic, has been turned into something as hard and durable as a geometrical figure itself.

The word machinery here suggests to me a point which requires a short discussion. You admit here this change of sensibility. You find the artists seeking out and using forms

and surfaces which artists of our immediate
past have always shrunk from. What is the
cause of this change of sensibility? Any
one who has agreed with the historical part
of this paper will probably agree that this
change of sensibility follows from a certain
change in intention in art, the tendency
towards abstraction instead of towards empathy. But another explanation may be
given which, while it has an appearance of
making the thing reasonable, seems to me to
be fallacious. It may be said that an artist
is using mechanical lines because he lives in
an environment of machinery. In a landscape you would use softer and more organic
lines. This seems to me to be using the
materialist explanation of the origin of an art
which has been generally rejected. Take the
analogous case of the influence of raw material
on art. The nature of material is never without a certain influence. If they had not been
able to use granite, the Egyptians would
probably not have carved in the way they
did. But then the material did not produce
the style. If Egypt had been inhabited by
people of Greek race, the fact that the material
was granite, would not have made them produce anything like Egyptian sculpture. The
technical qualities of a material can thus
never create a style. A feeling for form of a
certain kind must always be the source of an
art. All that can be said of the forms suggested by the technical qualities of the

108

material is that they must not contradict this intended form. They can only be used when the inclination and taste to which they are appropriate already exist. So, though steel is not the material of the new art, but only its environment, we can, it seems to me, legitimately speak of it exercising the kind of influence that the use of granite did on Egyptian art, no more and no less.

The point I want to emphasise is that the use of mechanical lines in the new art is in no sense merely a reflection of mechanical environment. It is a result of a change of sensibility which is, I think, the result of a change of attitude which will become increasingly obvious.

Finally I think that this association with the idea of machinery takes away any kind of dilettante character from the movement and makes it seem more solid and more inevitable.

It seems to me beyond doubt that this, whether you like it or not, is the character of the art that is coming. I speak of it myself with enthusiasm, not only because I appreciate it for itself, but because I believe it to be the precursor of a much wider change in philosophy and general outlook on the world.

ROMANTICISM
AND CLASSICISM

ROMANTICISM AND CLASSICISM

I WANT to maintain that after a hundred years of romanticism, we are in for a classical revival, and that the particular weapon of this new classical spirit, when it works in verse, will be fancy. And in this I imply the superiority of fancy—not superior generally or absolutely, for that would be obvious nonsense, but superior in the sense that we use the word good in empirical ethics—good for something, superior for something. I shall have to prove then two things, first that a classical revival is coming, and, secondly, for its particular purposes, fancy will be superior to imagination.

So banal have the terms Imagination and Fancy become that we imagine they must have always been in the language. Their history as two differing terms in the vocabulary of criticism is comparatively short. Originally, of course, they both mean the same thing ; they first began to be differentiated by the German writers on æsthetics in the eighteenth century.

I know that in using the words " classic " and " romantic " I am doing a dangerous thing. They represent five or six different kinds of antitheses, and while I may be using them in one sense you may be interpreting them in another. In this present connection I am using them in a perfectly precise and limited sense. I ought really to have coined a couple of new words, but I prefer to use the ones I have used, as I then conform to the practice of the group of polemical writers who make most use of them at the present day, and have almost succeeded in making them political catchwords. I mean Maurras, Lasserre and all the group connected with *L'Action Française.*

At the present time this is the particular group with which the distinction is most vital. Because it has become a party symbol. If you asked a man of a certain set whether he preferred the classics or the romantics, you could deduce from that what his politics were.

The best way of gliding into a proper definition of my terms would be to start with a set of people who are prepared to fight about it—for in them you will have no vagueness. (Other people take the infamous attitude of the person with catholic tastes who says he likes both.)

About a year ago, a man whose name I think was Fauchois gave a lecture at the Odéon on Racine, in the course of which he made some disparaging remarks about his dullness, lack of invention and the rest of it. This caused an immediate riot : fights took place all over the house ; several people were arrested and imprisoned, and the rest of the series of lectures took place with hundreds of gendarmes and detectives scattered all over the place. These people interrupted because the classical ideal is a living thing to them and Racine is the great classic. That is what I call a real vital interest in literature. They regard romanticism as an awful disease from which France had just recovered.

The thing is complicated in their case by the fact that it was romanticism that made the revolution. They hate the revolution, so they hate romanticism.

I make no apology for dragging in politics here ; romanticism both in England and France is associated with certain political views, and it is in taking a concrete example of the working out of a principle in action that you can get its best definition.

What was the positive principle behind all the other principles of '89 ? I am talking here of the revolution in as far as it was an idea ; I leave out material causes—they only produce the forces. The barriers which could easily have resisted or guided these forces had been previously rotted away by ideas. This always seems to be the case in successful changes ; the privileged class is beaten only when it has lost faith in itself, when it has itself been penetrated with the ideas which are working against it.

It was not the rights of man—that was a

good solid practical war-cry. The thing which created enthusiasm, which made the revolution practically a new religion, was something more positive than that. People of all classes, people who stood to lose by it, were in a positive ferment about the idea of liberty. There must have been some idea which enabled them to think that something positive could come out of so essentially negative a thing. There was, and here I get my definition of romanticism. They had been taught by Rousseau that man was by nature good, that it was only bad laws and customs that had suppressed him. Remove all these and the infinite possibilities of man would have a chance. This is what made them think that something positive could come out of disorder, this is what created the religious enthusiasm. Here is the root of all romanticism : that man, the individual, is an infinite reservoir of possibilities ; and if you can so rearrange society by the destruction of oppressive order then these possibilities will have a chance and you will get Progress.

One can define the classical quite clearly as the exact opposite to this. Man is an extraordinarily fixed and limited animal whose nature is absolutely constant. It is only by tradition and organisation that anything decent can be got out of him.

This view was a little shaken at the time of Darwin. You remember his particular hypothesis, that new species came into existence by the cumulative effect of small variations— this seems to admit the possibility of future progress. But at the present day the contrary hypothesis makes headway in the shape of De Vries's mutation theory, that each new species comes into existence, not gradually by the accumulation of small steps, but suddenly in a jump, a kind of sport, and that once in existence it remains absolutely fixed. This enables me to keep the classical view with an appearance of scientific backing.

Put shortly, these are the two views, then. One, that man is intrinsically good, spoilt by circumstance ; and the other that he is intrinsically limited, but disciplined by order and tradition to something fairly decent. To the one party man's nature is like a well, to the other like a bucket. The view which regards man as a well, a reservoir full of possibilities, I call the romantic ; the one which regards him as a very finite and fixed creature, I call the classical.

One may note here that the Church has always taken the classical view since the defeat of the Pelagian heresy and the adoption of the sane classical dogma of original sin.

It would be a mistake to identify the classical view with that of materialism. On the contrary it is absolutely identical with the normal religious attitude. I should put it in this way : That part of the fixed nature of man is the belief in the Deity. This should be as fixed and true for every man as belief in the existence of matter and in the objective world. It is parallel to appetite, the instinct of sex, and all the other fixed qualities. Now at certain times, by the use of either force or rhetoric, these instincts have been suppressed —in Florence under Savonarola, in Geneva under Calvin, and here under the Round-heads. The inevitable result of such a process is that the repressed instinct bursts out in some abnormal direction. So with religion. By the perverted rhetoric of Rationalism, your natural instincts are suppressed and you are converted into an agnostic. Just as in the case of the other instincts, Nature has her revenge. The instincts that find their right and proper outlet in religion must come out in some other way. You don't believe in a God, so you begin to believe that man is a god. You don't believe in Heaven, so you begin to believe in a heaven on earth. In other words, you get romanticism. The concepts that are right and proper in their own sphere are spread over, and so mess up, falsify and blur the clear outlines of human experience. It is like pouring a pot of treacle over the dinner table. Romanticism then, and this is the best definition I can give of it, is spilt religion.

I must now shirk the difficulty of saying exactly what I mean by romantic and classical in verse. I can only say that it means the result of these two attitudes towards the cosmos, towards man, in so far as it gets reflected in verse. The romantic, because he thinks man infinite, must always be talking about the infinite ; and as there is always the bitter contrast between what you think you ought to be able to do and what man actually can, it always tends, in its later stages at any rate, to be gloomy. I really can't go any further than to say it is the reflection of these two temperaments, and point out examples of the different spirits. On the one hand I would take such diverse people as Horace, most of the Elizabethans and the writers of the Augustan age, and on the other side Lamartine, Hugo, parts of Keats, Coleridge, Byron, Shelley and Swinburne.

I know quite well that when people think of classical and romantic in verse, the contrast at once comes into their mind between, say, Racine and Shakespeare. I don't mean this ; the dividing line that I intend is here misplaced a little from the true middle. That Racine is on the extreme classical side I agree, but if you call Shakespeare romantic, you are using a different definition to the one I give. You are thinking of the difference between classic and romantic as being merely one between restraint and exuberance. I should say with Nietzsche that there are two kinds of classicism, the static and the dynamic. Shakespeare is the classic of motion.

What I mean by classical in verse, then, is this. That even in the most imaginative flights there is always a holding back, a reservation. The classical poet never forgets this finiteness, this limit of man. He remembers always that he is mixed up with earth. He may jump, but he always returns back ; he never flies away into the circumambient gas.

You might say if you wished that the whole of the romantic attitude seems to crystallise in verse round metaphors of flight. Hugo is always flying, flying over abysses, flying up into the eternal gases. The word infinite in every other line.

In the classical attitude you never seem to swing right along to the infinite nothing. If you say an extravagant thing which does exceed the limits inside which you know man to be fastened, yet there is always conveyed in some way at the end an impression of yourself standing outside it, and not quite believing it, or consciously putting it forward as a flourish. You never go blindly into an atmosphere more than the truth, an atmosphere too rarefied for man to breathe for long. You are always faithful to the conception of a limit. It is a question of pitch ; in romantic verse you move at a certain pitch of rhetoric which you know, man being what he is, to be a little high-falutin. The kind of thing you get in Hugo or Swinburne. In the coming classical reaction that will feel just wrong. For an example of the opposite thing, a verse written in the proper classical spirit, I can

take the song from Cymbeline beginning with
" Fear no more the heat of the sun." I am
just using this as a parable. I don't quite
mean what I say here. Take the last two
lines :

> "Golden lads and girls all must,
> Like chimney sweepers come to dust."

Now, no romantic would have ever written
that. Indeed, so ingrained is romanticism,
so objectionable is this to it, that people have
asserted that these were not part of the
original song.

Apart from the pun, the thing that I think
quite classical is the word lad. Your modern
romantic could never write that. He would
have to write golden youth, and take up the
thing at least a couple of notes in pitch.

I want now to give the reasons which make
me think that we are nearing the end of the
romantic movement.

The first lies in the nature of any convention
or tradition in art. A particular convention or
attitude in art has a strict analogy to the
phenomena of organic life. It grows old and
decays. It has a definite period of life and
must die. All the possible tunes get played
on it and then it is exhausted ; moreover
its best period is its youngest. Take the case
of the extraordinary efflorescence of verse in
the Elizabethan period. All kinds of reasons
have been given for this—the discovery of the
new world and all the rest of it. There is a
much simpler one. A new medium had been

given them to play with—namely, blank verse. It was new and so it was easy to play new tunes on it.

The same law holds in other arts. All the masters of painting are born into the world at a time when the particular tradition from which they start is imperfect. The Florentine tradition was just short of full ripeness when Raphael came to Florence, the Bellinesque was still young when Titian was born in Venice. Landscape was still a toy or an appanage of figure-painting when Turner and Constable arose to reveal its independent power. When Turner and Constable had done with landscape they left little or nothing for their successors to do on the same lines. Each field of artistic activity is exhausted by the first great artist who gathers a full harvest from it.

This period of exhaustion seems to me to have been reached in romanticism. We shall not get any new efflorescence of verse until we get a new technique, a new convention, to turn ourselves loose in.

Objection might be taken to this. It might be said that a century as an organic unity doesn't exist, that I am being deluded by a wrong metaphor, that I am treating a collection of literary people as if they were an organism or state department. Whatever we may be in other things, an objector might urge, in literature in as far as we are anything at all— in as far as we are worth considering—we are individuals, we are persons, and as distinct persons we cannot be subordinated to any general treatment. At any period at any time, an individual poet may be a classic or a romantic just as he feels like it. You at any particular moment may think that you can stand outside a movement. You may think that as an individual you observe both the classic and the romantic spirit and decide from a purely detached point of view that one is superior to the other.

The answer to this is that no one, in a matter of judgment of beauty, can take a detached standpoint in this way. Just as physically you are not born that abstract entity, man, but the child of particular parents, so you are in matters of literary judgment. Your opinion is almost entirely of the literary history that came just before you, and you are governed by that whatever you may think. Take Spinoza's example of a stone falling to the ground. If it had a conscious mind it would, he said, think it was going to the ground because it wanted to. So you with your pretended free judgment about what is and what is not beautiful. The amount of freedom in man is much exaggerated. That we are free on certain rare occasions, both my religion and the views I get from metaphysics convince me. But many acts which we habitually label free are in reality automatic. It is quite possible for a man to write a book almost automatically.

I have read several such products. Some observations were recorded more than twenty years ago by Robertson on reflex speech, and he found that in certain cases of dementia, where the people were quite unconscious so far as the exercise of reasoning went, that very intelligent answers were given to a succession of questions on politics and such matters. The meaning of these questions could not possibly have been understood. Language here acted after the manner of a reflex. So that certain extremely complex mechanisms, subtle enough to imitate beauty, can work by themselves—I certainly think that this is the case with judgments about beauty.

I can put the same thing in slightly different form. Here is a question of a conflict of two attitudes, as it might be of two techniques. The critic, while he has to admit that changes from one to the other occur, persists in regarding them as mere variations to a certain fixed normal, just as a pendulum might swing. I admit the analogy of the pendulum as far as movement, but I deny the further consequence of the analogy, the existence of the point of rest, the normal point.

When I say that I dislike the romantics, I dissociate two things : the part of them in which they resemble all the great poets, and the part in which they differ and which gives them their character as romantics. It is this minor element which constitutes the particular note of a century, and which, while it excites contemporaries, annoys the next generation. It was precisely that quality in Pope which pleased his friends, which we detest. Now, anyone just before the romantics who felt that, could have predicted that a change was coming. It seems to me that we stand just in the same position now. I think that there is an increasing proportion of people who simply can't stand Swinburne.

When I say that there will be another classical revival I don't necessarily anticipate a return to Pope. I say merely that now is the time for such a revival. Given people of the necessary capacity, it may be a vital thing ; without them we may get a formalism something like Pope. When it does come we may not even recognise it as classical. Although it will be classical it will be different because it has passed through a romantic period. To take a parallel example : I remember being very surprised, after seeing the Post Impressionists, to find in Maurice Denis's account of the matter that they consider themselves classical in the sense that they were trying to impose the same order on the mere flux of new material provided by the impressionist movement, that existed in the more limited materials of the painting before.

There is something now to be cleared away before I get on with my argument, which is that while romanticism is dead in reality, yet the critical attitude appropriate to it still continues to exist. To make this a little clearer : For every kind of verse, there is a corresponding receptive attitude. In a romantic period we demand from verse certain qualities. In a classical period we demand others. At the present time I should say that this receptive attitude has outlasted the thing from which it was formed. But while the romantic tradition has run dry, yet the critical attitude of mind, which demands romantic qualities from verse, still survives. So that if good classical verse were to be written to-morrow very few people would be able to stand it.

I object even to the best of the romantics. I object still more to the receptive attitude. I object to the sloppiness which doesn't consider that a poem is a poem unless it is moaning or whining about something or other. I always think in this connection of the last line of a poem of John Webster's which ends with a request I cordially endorse :

"End your moan and come away."

The thing has got so bad now that a poem which is all dry and hard, a properly classical poem, would not be considered poetry at all. How many people now can lay their hands on their hearts and say they like either Horace or Pope? They feel a kind of chill when they read them.

The dry hardness which you get in the

classics is absolutely repugnant to them. Poetry that isn't damp isn't poetry at all. They cannot see that accurate description is a legitimate object of verse. Verse to them always means a bringing in of some of the emotions that are grouped round the word infinite.

The essence of poetry to most people is that it must lead them to a beyond of some kind. Verse strictly confined to the earthly and the definite (Keats is full of it) might seem to them to be excellent writing, excellent craftsmanship, but not poetry. So much has romanticism debauched us, that, without some form of vagueness, we deny the highest.

In the classic it is always the light of ordinary day, never the light that never was on land or sea. It is always perfectly human and never exaggerated : man is always man and never a god.

But the awful result of romanticism is that, accustomed to this strange light, you can never live without it. Its effect on you is that of a drug.

There is a general tendency to think that verse means little else than the expression of unsatisfied emotion. People say : " But how can you have verse without sentiment ? " You see what it is : the prospect alarms them. A classical revival to them would mean the prospect of an arid desert and the death of poetry as they understand it, and could only come to fill the gap caused by that death. Exactly why this dry classical spirit should have a positive and legitimate necessity to express itself in poetry is utterly inconceivable to them. What this positive need is, I shall show later. It follows from the fact that there is another quality, not the emotion produced, which is at the root of excellence in verse. Before I get to this I am concerned with a negative thing, a theoretical point, a prejudice that stands in the way and is really at the bottom of this reluctance to understand classical verse.

It is an objection which ultimately I believe comes from a bad metaphysic of art. You are unable to admit the existence of beauty without the infinite being in some way or another dragged in.

I may quote for purposes of argument, as a typical example of this kind of attitude made vocal, the famous chapters in Ruskin's *Modern Painters*, Vol. II, on the imagination. I must say here, parenthetically, that I use this word without prejudice to the other discussion with which I shall end the paper. I only use the word here because it is Ruskin's word. All that I am concerned with just now is the attitude behind it, which I take to be the romantic.

" Imagination cannot but be serious ; she sees too far, too darkly, too solemnly, too earnestly, ever to smile. There is something in the heart of everything, if we can reach it, that we shall not be inclined to laugh at. . . .

Those who have so pierced and seen the melancholy deeps of things, are filled with intense passion and gentleness of sympathy." (Part III, Chap. III, § 9.)

" There is in every word set down by the imaginative mind an awful undercurrent of meaning, and evidence and shadow upon it of the deep places out of which it has come. It is often obscure, often half-told ; for he who wrote it, in his clear seeing of the things beneath, may have been impatient of detailed interpretation ; for if we choose to dwell upon it and trace it, it will lead us always securely back to that metropolis of the soul's dominion from which we may follow out all the ways and tracks to its farthest coasts." (Part III, Chap. III, § 5.)

Really in all these matters the act of judgment is an instinct, an absolutely unstateable thing akin to the art of the tea taster. But you must talk, and the only language you can use in this matter is that of analogy. I have no material clay to mould to the given shape ; the only thing which one has for the purpose, and which acts as a substitute for it, a kind of mental clay, are certain metaphors modified into theories of æsthetic and rhetoric. A combination of these, while it cannot state the essentially unstateable intuition, can yet give you a sufficient analogy to enable you to see what it was and to recognise it on condition that you yourself have been in a similar state. Now these phrases of Ruskin's convey quite clearly to me his taste in the matter.

I see quite clearly that he thinks the best verse must be serious. That is a natural attitude for a man in the romantic period. But he is not content with saying that he prefers this kind of verse. He wants to deduce his opinion like his master, Coleridge, from some fixed principle which can be found by metaphysic.

Here is the last refuge of this romantic attitude. It proves itself to be not an attitude but a deduction from a fixed principle of the cosmos.

One of the main reasons for the existence of philosophy is not that it enables you to find truth (it can never do that) but that it does provide you a refuge for definitions. The usual idea of the thing is that it provides you with a fixed basis from which you can deduce the things you want in æsthetics. The process is the exact contrary. You start in the confusion of the fighting line, you retire from that just a little to the rear to recover, to get your weapons right. Quite plainly, without metaphor this—it provides you with an elaborate and precise language in which you really can explain definitely what you mean, but what you want to say is decided by other things. The ultimate reality is the hurly-burly, the struggle ; the metaphysic is an adjunct to clear-headedness in it.

To get back to Ruskin and his objection

to all that is not serious. It seems to me that involved in this is a bad metaphysical æsthetic. You have the metaphysic which in defining beauty or the nature of art always drags in the infinite. Particularly in Germany, the land where theories of æsthetics were first created, the romantic æsthetes collated all beauty to an impression of the infinite involved in the identification of our being in absolute spirit. In the least element of beauty we have a total intuition of the whole world. Every artist is a kind of pantheist.

Now it is quite obvious to anyone who holds this kind of theory that any poetry which confines itself to the finite can never be of the highest kind. It seems a contradiction in terms to them. And as in metaphysics you get the last refuge of a prejudice, so it is now necessary for me to refute this.

Here follows a tedious piece of dialectic, but it is necessary for my purpose. I must avoid two pitfalls in discussing the idea of beauty. On the one hand there is the old classical view which is supposed to define it as lying in conformity to certain standard fixed forms ; and on the other hand there is the romantic view which drags in the infinite. I have got to find a metaphysic between these two which will enable me to hold consistently that a neo-classic verse of the type I have indicated involves no contradiction in terms. It is essential to prove that beauty may be in small, dry things.

131

The great aim is accurate, precise and definite description. The first thing is to recognise how extraordinarily difficult this is. It is no mere matter of carefulness ; you have to use language, and language is by its very nature a communal thing ; that is, it expresses never the exact thing but a compromise—that which is common to you, me and everybody. But each man sees a little differently, and to get out clearly and exactly what he does see, he must have a terrific struggle with language, whether it be with words or the technique of other arts. Language has its own special nature, its own conventions and communal ideas. It is only by a concentrated effort of the mind that you can hold it fixed to your own purpose. I always think that the fundamental process at the back of all the arts might be represented by the following metaphor.* You know what I call architect's curves—flat pieces of wood with all different kinds of curvature. By a suitable selection from these you can draw approximately any curve you like. The artist I take to be the man who simply can't bear the idea of that ' approximately.' He will get the exact curve of what he sees whether it be an object or an idea in the mind. I shall here have to change my metaphor a little to get the process in his

* [This metaphor is used elsewhere by Hulme—in dealing with Bergson's Theory of Art (p. 160 *infra*)—but I have refrained from deleting it here because of its particular relevancy. —H. R.]

mind. Suppose that instead of your curved pieces of wood you have a springy piece of steel of the same types of curvature as the wood. Now the state of tension or concentration of mind, if he is doing anything really good in this struggle against the ingrained habit of the technique, may be represented by a man employing all his fingers to bend the steel out of its own curve and into the exact curve which you want. Something different to what it would assume naturally.

There are then two things to distinguish, first the particular faculty of mind to see things as they really are, and apart from the conventional ways in which you have been trained to see them. This is itself rare enough in all consciousness. Second, the concentrated state of mind, the grip over oneself which is necessary in the actual expression of what one sees. To prevent one falling into the conventional curves of ingrained technique, to hold on through infinite detail and trouble to the exact curve you want. Wherever you get this sincerity, you get the fundamental quality of good art without dragging in infinite or serious.

I can now get at that positive fundamental quality of verse which constitutes excellence, which has nothing to do with infinity, with mystery or with emotions.

This is the point I aim at, then, in my argument. I prophesy· that a period of dry, hard, classical verse is coming. I have met the preliminary objection founded on the bad romantic æsthetic that in such verse, from which the infinite is excluded, you cannot have the essence of poetry at all.

After attempting to sketch out what this positive quality is, I can get on to the end of my paper in this way : That where you get this quality exhibited in the realm of the emotions you get imagination, and that where you get this quality exhibited in the contemplation of finite things you get fancy.

In prose as in algebra concrete things are embodied in signs or counters which are moved about according to rules, without being visualised at all in the process. There are in prose certain type situations and arrangements of words, which move as automatically into certain other arrangements as do functions in algebra. One only changes the X's and the Y's back into physical things at the end of the process. Poetry, in one aspect at any rate, may be considered as an effort to avoid this characteristic of prose. It is not a counter language, but a visual concrete one. It is a compromise for a language of intuition which would hand over sensations bodily. It always endeavours to arrest you, and to make you continuously see a physical thing, to prevent you gliding through an abstract process. It chooses fresh epithets and fresh metaphors, not so much because they are new, and we are tired of the old, but because the old cease to convey a

physical thing and become abstract counters.
A poet says a ship ' coursed the seas ' to get a
physical image, instead of the counter word
' sailed.' Visual meanings can only be transferred by the new bowl of metaphor ; prose
is an old pot that lets them leak out. Images
in verse are not mere decoration, but the very
essence of an intuitive language. Verse is a
pedestrian taking you over the ground, prose
—a train which delivers you at a destination.

I can now get on to a discussion of two
words often used in this connection, " fresh "
and " unexpected." You praise a thing for
being " fresh." I understand what you mean,
but the word besides conveying the truth
conveys a secondary something which is
certainly false. When you say a poem or
drawing is fresh, and so good, the impression
is somehow conveyed that the essential element of goodness is freshness, that it is good
because it is fresh. Now this is certainly
wrong, there is nothing particularly desirable
about freshness *per se*. Works of art aren't
eggs. Rather the contrary. It is simply
an unfortunate necessity due to the nature of
language and technique that the only way the
element which does constitute goodness, the
only way in which its presence can be de-
tected externally, is by freshness. Freshness
convinces you, you feel at once that the
artist was in an actual physical state. You
feel that for a minute. Real communication
is so very rare, for plain speech is uncon-

vincing. It is in this rare fact of communication that you get the root of æsthetic pleasure.

I shall maintain that wherever you get an extraordinary interest in a thing, a great zest in its contemplation which carries on the contemplator to accurate description in the sense of the word accurate I have just analysed, there you have sufficient justification for poetry. It must be an intense zest which heightens a thing out of the level of prose. I am using contemplation here just in the same way that Plato used it, only applied to a different subject ; it is a detached interest. " The object of æsthetic contemplation is something framed apart by itself and regarded without memory or expectation, simply as being itself, as end not means, as individual not universal."

To take a concrete example. I am taking an extreme case. If you are walking behind a woman in the street, you notice the curious way in which the skirt rebounds from her heels. If that peculiar kind of motion becomes of such interest to you that you will search about until you can get the exact epithet which hits it off, there you have a properly æsthetic emotion. But it is the zest with which you look at the thing which decides you to make the effort. In this sense the feeling that was in Herrick's mind when he wrote " the tempestuous petticoat " was exactly the same as that which in bigger and vaguer matters makes the best romantic verse.

It doesn't matter an atom that the emotion produced is not of dignified vagueness, but on the contrary amusing ; the point is that exactly the same activity is at work as in the highest verse. That is the avoidance of conventional language in order to get the exact curve of the thing.

I have still to show that in the verse which is to come, fancy will be the necessary weapon of the classical school. The positive quality I have talked about can be manifested in ballad verse by extreme directness and simplicity, such as you get in "On Fair Kirkconnel Lea." But the particular verse we are going to get will be cheerful, dry and sophisticated, and here the necessary weapon of the positive quality must be fancy.

Subject doesn't matter ; the quality in it is the same as you get in the more romantic people.

It isn't the scale or kind of emotion produced that decides, but this one fact : Is there any real zest in it ? Did the poet have an actually realised visual object before him in which he delighted ? It doesn't matter if it were a lady's shoe or the starry heavens.

Fancy is not mere decoration added on to plain speech. Plain speech is essentially inaccurate. It is only by new metaphors, that is, by fancy, that it can be made precise.

When the analogy has not enough connection with the thing described to be quite parallel with it, where it overlays the thing it described and there is a certain excess, there you have the play of fancy—that I grant is inferior to imagination.

But where the analogy is every bit of it necessary for accurate description in the sense of the word accurate I have previously described, and your only objection to this kind of fancy is that it is not serious in the effect it produces, then I think the objection to be entirely invalid. If it is sincere in the accurate sense, when the whole of the analogy is necessary to get out the exact curve of the feeling or thing you want to express—there you seem to me to have the highest verse, even though the subject be trivial and the emotions of the infinite far away.

It is very difficult to use any terminology at all for this kind of thing. For whatever word you use is at once sentimentalised. Take Coleridge's word " vital." It is used loosely by all kinds of people who talk about art, to mean something vaguely and mysteriously significant. In fact, vital and mechanical is to them exactly the same antithesis as between good and bad.

Nothing of the kind ; Coleridge uses it in a perfectly definite and what I call dry sense. It is just this : A mechanical complexity is the sum of its parts. Put them side by side and you get the whole. Now vital or organic is merely a convenient metaphor for a complexity of a different kind, that in which the parts cannot be said to be elements as each one is modified by the other's presence, and each one to a certain extent is the whole. The leg of a chair by itself is still a leg. My leg by itself wouldn't be.

Now the characteristic of the intellect is that it can only represent complexities of the mechanical kind. It can only make diagrams, and diagrams are essentially things whose parts are separate one from another. The intellect always analyses—when there is a synthesis it is baffled. That is why the artist's work seems mysterious. The intellect can't represent it. This is a necessary consequence of the particular nature of the intellect and the purposes for which it is formed. It doesn't mean that your synthesis is ineffable, simply that it can't be definitely stated.

Now this is all worked out in Bergson, the central feature of his whole philosophy. It is all based on the clear conception of these vital complexities which he calls "intensive" as opposed to the other kind which he calls "extensive," and the recognition of the fact that the intellect can only deal with the extensive multiplicity. To deal with the intensive you must use intuition.

Now, as I said before, Ruskin was perfectly aware of all this, but he had no such metaphysical background which would enable him to state definitely what he meant. The result is that he has to flounder about in a series of metaphors. A powerfully imaginative mind seizes and combines at the same instant all the important ideas of its poem or picture, and while it works with one of them, it is at the same instant working with and modifying all in their relation to it and never losing sight of their bearings on each other— as the motion of a snake's body goes through all parts at once and its volition acts at the same instant in coils which go contrary ways.

A romantic movement must have an end of the very nature of the thing. It may be deplored, but it can't be helped—wonder must cease to be wonder.

I guard myself here from all the consequences of the analogy, but it expresses at any rate the inevitableness of the process. A literature of wonder must have an end as inevitably as a strange land loses its strangeness when one lives in it. Think of the lost ecstasy of the Elizabethans. " Oh my America, my new found land," think of what it meant to them and of what it means to us. Wonder can only be the attitude of a man passing from one stage to another, it can never be a permanently fixed thing.

BERGSON'S THEORY
OF ART

BERGSON'S THEORY OF ART

1. THE great difficulty in any talk about art lies in the extreme indefiniteness of the vocabulary you are obliged to employ. The concepts by which you endeavour to describe your attitude toward any work of art are so extraordinarily fluid. Words like creative, expressive, vital, rhythm, unity and personality are so vague that you can never be sure when you use them that you are conveying over at all the meaning you intended to. This is constantly realised unconsciously ; in almost every decade a new catch word is invented which for a few years after its invention does convey, to a small set of people at any rate, a definite meaning, but even that very soon lapses into a fluid condition when it means anything and nothing.

This leads me to the point of view which I take about Bergson in relation to art. He has not created any new theory of art. That would be absurd. But what he does seem to me to have done is that by the acute analysis of certain mental processes he has enabled us to state more definitely and with less distortion the qualities which we feel in art.

2. The finished portrait is explained by the features of the model, by the nature of the artist, by the colours spread out of the palette ; but even with the knowledge of what explains it, no one, not even the artist, could have foreseen exactly what the portrait would be. For to predict it would be to produce it before it was produced. Creation in art is not necessarily a mere synthesis of elements. In so far as we are geometricians we reject the unforeseeable. We might accept it assuredly in so far as we are artists, for art lives on creation and implies a belief in the spontaneity of nature. But disinterested art is a luxury like pure speculation. Our eye perceives the features of the living being merely as assembled, not as mutually organised. The intention of life—a simple movement which runs through the lines and binds them together and gives them significance—escapes it. This intention is just what the artist tries to regain in placing himself back within the object by a kind of sympathy and breaking down by an effort of intuition the barrier that space puts between him and his model. It is true that this æsthetic intuition, like external perception, only attains the individual, but we can conceive an inquiry turned in the same direction as art which would take life in general for its object just as physical science, following to the end the direction pointed out by external perception, prolongs the individual facts into general laws.

3. In the state of mind produced in you by any work of art there must necessarily be a rather complicated mixture of the emotions. Among these is one which can properly be called an essentially æsthetic emotion. It could not occur alone, isolated ; it may only constitute a small proportion of the total emotion produced ; but it is, as far as any investigation in the nature of æsthetics is concerned, the important thing. In the total body of effect produced by music, nine-tenths may be an effect which, properly speaking, is independent of the essentially æsthetic emotion which we get from it. The same thing is most obviously true of painting. The total effect produced by any painting is most obviously a composite thing composed of a great many different kinds of emotions— the pleasure one gets from the subject, from the quality of the colour and the painting, and then the subsidiary pleasures one gets from recognition of the style, of a period or a particular painter. Mixed up with these is the one, sometimes small element of emotion, which is the veritable æsthetic one.

4. In order to be able to state the nature of the process which I think is involved in any art, I have had to use a certain kind of voca-bulary, to postulate certain things. I have had to suppose a reality of infinite variability, and one that escapes all the stock perceptions, without being able to give any actual account of that reality. I have had to suppose that

human perception gets crystallised out along certain lines, that it has certain fixed habits, certain fixed ways of seeing things, and is so unable to see things as they are.

Putting the thing generally—I have had to make all kinds of suppositions simply and solely for the purpose of being able to convey over and state the nature of the activity you get in art. Now the extraordinary importance of Bergson for any theory of art is that, starting with a different aim altogether, seeking merely to give an account of reality, he arrives at certain conclusions as being true, and these conclusions are the very things which we had to suppose in order to give an account of art. The advantage of this is that it removes your account of art from the merely literary level, from the level at which it is a more or less successful attempt to describe what you feel about the matter, and enables you to state it as an account of actual reality.

5. The two parts of Bergson's general philosophical position which are important in the theory of æsthetic are (1) the conception of reality as a flux of interpenetrated elements unseizable by the intellect (this gives a more precise meaning to the word reality which has been employed so often in the previous pages, when art has been defined as a more direct communication of reality) ; and (2) his account of the part played in the development of the ordinary characteristics

146

of the mind by its orientation towards action. This in its turn enables one to give a more coherent account of the reason for what previously has only been assumed, the fact that in ordinary perception, both of external objects and of our internal states, we never perceive things as they are, but only certain conventional types.

6. Man's primary need is not *knowledge* but *action*. The characteristic of the intellect itself Bergson deduces from this fact. The function of the intellect is so to present things not that we may most thoroughly understand them, but that we may successfully act on them. Everything in man is dominated by his necessity of action.

7. The creative activity of the artist is only necessary because of the limitations placed on internal and external perception by the necessities of action. If we could break through the veil which action interposes, if we could come into direct contact with sense and consciousness, art would be useless and unnecessary. Our eyes, aided by memory, would carve out in space and fix in time the most inimitable of pictures. In the centre of one's own mind, we should hear constantly a certain music. But as this is impossible, the function of the artist is to pierce through here and there, accidentally as it were, the veil placed between us and reality by the limitations of our perception engendered by action.

8. Philosophers are always giving definitions

of art with which the artist, when he is not actively working but merely talking after dinner, is content to agree with, because it puts his function in some grandiose phraseology which he finds rather flattering. I remember hearing Mr Rothenstein in an after-dinner speech say that " art was the *revelation of the infinite in the finite.*" I am very far from suggesting that he invented that phrase, but I quote it as showing that he evidently felt that it did convey something of the matter. And so it does in a way, but it is so hopelessly vague. It may convey the kind of excitement which art may produce in you, but it in no way fits the actual process that the artist goes through. It defines art in much the same way that saying that I was in Europe would define my position in space. It includes art, but it gives you no specific description of it.

This kind of thing was not dangerous to the artists themselves, because being familiar with the specific thing intended they were able to discount all the rest. When the infinite in the finite was mentioned, they knew the quite specific and limited quality which was intended. The danger comes from the outsiders who, not knowing, not being familiar with the specific quality, take words like infinite in the much bigger sense than is really intended.

9. To describe the nature of the activity you get in art, the philosopher must always create some kind of special vocabulary. He

has to make use of certain metaphysical conceptions in order to state the thing satisfactorily. The great advantage of Bergson's theory is that it states the thing most nakedly, with the least amount of metaphysical baggage. In essence, of course, his theory is exactly the same as Schopenhauer's. That is, they both want to convey over the same feeling about art. But Schopenhauer demands such a cumbrous machinery in order to get that feeling out. Art is the pure contemplation of the Idea in a moment of emancipation from the Will. To state a quite simple thing he has to invent two very extraordinary ones. In Bergson it is an actual contact with reality in a man who is emancipated from the ways of perception engendered by action, but the action is written with a small " a," not a large one.

10. The process of artistic creation would be better described as a process of discovery and disentanglement. To use the metaphor which one is by now so familiar with—the stream of the inner life, and the definite crystallised shapes on the surface—the big artist, the creative artist, the innovator, leaves the level where things are crystallised out into these definite shapes, and, diving down into the inner flux, comes back with a new shape which he endeavours to fix. He cannot be said to have created it, but to have discovered it, because when he has definitely expressed it we recognise it as true. Great painters

are men in whom has originated a certain
vision of things which has become or will
become the vision of everybody. Once the
painter has seen it, it becomes easy for all of
us to see it. A mould has been made. But
the creative activity came in the effort which
was necessary to disentangle this particular
type of vision from the general haze—the
effort, that is, which is necessary to break
moulds and to make new ones. For instance,
the effect produced by Constable on the
English and French Schools of landscape
painting. Nobody before Constable saw
things, or at any rate painted them, in that
particular way. This makes it easier to see
clearly what one means by an individual way
of looking at things. It does not mean something which is peculiar to an individual, for
in that case it would be quite valueless. It
means that a certain individual artist was
able to break through the conventional ways
of looking at things which veil reality from us
at a certain point, was able to pick out one
element which is really in all of us, but which
before he had disentangled it, we were unable
to perceive. It is as if the surface of our
mind was a sea in a continual state of motion,
that there were so many waves on it, their
existence was so transient, and they interfered
so much with each other, that one was unable
to perceive them. The artist by making a
fixed model of one of these transient waves
enables you to isolate it out and to perceive

it in yourself. In that sense art merely reveals, it never creates.

11. Metaphors soon run their course and die. But it is necessary to remember that when they were first used by the poets who created them they were used for the purpose of conveying over a vividly felt actual sensation. Nothing could be more dead now than the conventional expressions of love poetry, the arrow which pierces the heart and the rest of it, but originally they were used as conveying over the reality of the sensation experienced.

12. If I say the hill is *clothed* with trees your mind simply runs past the word " clothed," it is not pulled up in any way to visualise it. You have no distinct image of the trees covering the hill as garments clothe the body. But if the trees had made a distinct impression on you when you saw them, if you were vividly interested in the effect they produced, you would probably not rest satisfied until you had got hold of some metaphor which did pull up the reader and make him visualise the thing. If there was only a narrow line of trees circling the hill near the top, you might say that it was *ruffed* with trees. I do not put this forward as a happy metaphor : I am only trying to get at the feeling which prompts this kind of expression. You have continually to be searching out new metaphors of this kind because the visual effect of a metaphor so soon dies. Even this word *clothed* which I

used was probably, the first time it was employed, an attempt on the part of a poet to convey over the vivid impression which the scene gave him. Every word in the language originates as a *live* metaphor, but gradually of course all visual meaning goes out of them and they become a kind of counters. Prose is in fact the museum where the dead metaphors of the poets are preserved.

The thing that concerns me here is of course only the *feeling* which is conveyed over to you by the use of fresh metaphors. It is only where you get these fresh metaphors and epithets employed that you get this vivid conviction which constitutes the purely æsthetic emotion that can be got from imagery.

13. From time to time in a fit of absent-mindedness nature raises up minds which are more detached from life—a natural detachment, one innate in the structure of sense or consciousness, which at once reveals itself by a virginal manner of seeing, hearing or thinking.

It is only by accident, and in one sense only, that nature produces someone whose perception is not riveted to practical purposes ; hence the diversity of the arts. One applies himself to form, not as it is practically useful in relation to him, but as it is in itself, as it reveals the inner life of things.

In our minds—behind the commonplace conventional expression which conceals emotion—artists attain the original mood and induce us to make the same effort ourselves by rhythmical arrangements of words, which, thus organised and animated with a life of their own, tell us, or rather suggest, things that speech is not calculated to express.

14. "*Art should endeavour to show the universal in the particular.*" This is a phrase that constantly recurs. I remember great play was made with it in Mr Binyon's little book on Chinese art. You are supposed to show, shining through the accidental qualities of the individual, the characteristics of a universal type. Of course this is perfectly correct if you give the words the right meaning. It seems at first sight to be the exact contrary to the definition that we have arrived at ourselves, which was that art must be always individual and springs from dissatisfaction with the generalised expressions of ordinary perception and ordinary language. The confusion simply springs from the two uses of the word " universal." To use Croce's example. Don Quixote is a type, but a type of what ? He is only a type of all the Don Quixotes. To use again my comparison of the curve, he is an accurately drawn representation of one of the individual curves that vary round the stock type which would be represented by the words loss of reality or love of glory. He is only universal in the sense that once having had that particular curve pointed out to you, you recognise it again.

15. From time to time, by a happy accident, men are born who either in one of their senses, or in their conscious life as a whole, are less dominated by the *necessities of action*. *Nature* has forgotten to attach their faculty for perception to their faculty for action. They do not perceive simply for the purposes of action : they perceive just for the sake of perceiving. It is necessary to point out here that this is taken in a profounder sense than the words are generally used. When one says that the mind is practical and that the artist is the person who is able to turn aside from action and to observe things as they are in a disinterested way, one should be careful to say that this does not refer to any conscious or controllable action. The words as they stand have almost a moral flavour. One might be understood as implying that one ought not to be so bound up in the practical. Of course the word *practical* is not used in this sense. It refers to something physiological and entirely beyond our control. This orientation of the mind towards action is the theory which is supposed to account for the characteristics of mental life itself, and is not a mere description of an avoidable and superficial habit of the individual mind.

When, therefore, you do get an artist, *i.e.* a man who either in one of his senses or in his mind generally is emancipated from this orientation of the mind towards action and is able to see things as they are in themselves, you are dealing with a rarity—a kind of accident produced by Nature itself and impossible of manufacture.

The artist is the man, then, who on one side of his nature is born detached from the necessities of action. According as this detachment is inherent in one or other of the senses or is inherent in the consciousness, he is painter, musician, or sculptor. If this detachment were complete—if the mind saw freshly and directly in every one of its methods of perception—then you would get a kind of artist such as the world has not yet seen. He would perceive all things in their native purity : the forms, sounds and colours of the physical world as well as the subtlest movements of the inner life. But this, of course, could never take place. All that you get is a breaking through of the surface-covering provided for things by the necessities of action in *one direction* only, *i.e.* in one *sense* only. Hence the diversity of the arts.

In one man it is the eye which is emancipated. He is able to see individual arrangements of line and colour which escape our standardised perceptions. And having perceived a hitherto unrecognised shape he is able gradually to insinuate it into our own perception. Others again retire within themselves. Beneath the conventional expression which hides the individual emotion they are able to see the original shape of it. They induce us to make the same effort ourselves and make us see what they see ; by rhythmical arrangements of words they tell us, or rather suggest, things that speech is not calculated to express.

Others get at emotions which have nothing in common with language ; certain rhythms of life at the centre of our minds. By setting free and emphasising this music they force it upon our attention : they compel us willy-nilly to fall in with it like passers-by who join in a dance.

In each art, then, the artist picks out of reality something which we, owing to a certain hardening of our perceptions, have been unable to see ourselves.

One might express the differences in the mechanism, by which they do this most easily, in terms of the metaphor by which we have previously expressed the difference between the two selves. Some arts proceed from the outside. They notice that the crystallised shapes on the top of the stream do not express the actual shapes on the waves. They endeavour to communicate the real shapes by adding detail. On the other hand, an art like music proceeds from *the inside* (as it were). By means of rhythm it breaks up the normal flow of our conscious life. It is as if by increasing the flow of the stream inside it broke through the surface crust and so made us realise the real nature of the outline of the inner elements of our conscious life. · It does this by means of rhythm which acts something like the means used to bring about the state of hypnosis. The rhythm and measure suspend the normal flow of our sensations by causing our attention to swing to and fro between fixed points and so take hold of us with such force that even the faintest imitation of sadness produces a great effect on us. It increases our sensibility, in fact.

16. What is the nature of the properly " æsthetic " emotion as distinct from the other emotions produced by art ?

As I have said, I do not think that Bergson has invented any new theory on this subject, but has simply created a much better vocabulary. That being so, I think that the best way to approach this theory is to state first the kind of rough conception which one had elaborated for oneself, and then to show how it is all straightened up in his analysis. By approaching the theory gradually in this way one can get it more solidly fixed down.

Among all the varied qualities of good verse, and in the complex kind of motion which it can produce, there is one quality it must possess, which can be easily separated from the other qualities and which constitutes this distinctively æsthetic emotion for which we are searching.

This peculiarly *æsthetic* emotion here, as in other arts, is overlaid with all kinds of other emotions and is only perceived by people who really understand verse. To get at what it is quite definitely, I only consider it in as far as it bears on the choice of epithets and images. The same quality is exhibited in the other parts of verse, in the rhythm and metre, for example, but it so happens that it is most easily isolated in the case of epithets.

17. Could reality come into direct contact with sense and consciousness, art would be useless, or rather we should all be artists. All these things that the artist sees exist, yet we do not see them—yet why not ?

Between nature and ourselves, even between ourselves and our own consciousness, there is a veil, a veil that is dense with the ordinary man, transparent for the artist and the poet. What made this veil ?

Life is action, it represents the acceptance of the utilitarian side of things in order to respond to them by appropriate actions. I look, I listen, I hear, I think I am seeing, I think I am hearing everything, and when I examine myself I think I am examining my own mind.

But I am not.

What I see and hear is simply a selection made by my senses to serve as a light for my conduct. My senses and my consciousness give me no more than a practical simplification of reality. In the usual perception I have of reality all the differences useless to man have been suppressed. My perception runs in certain moulds. Things have been classified with a view to the use I can make of them.

It is this classification I perceive rather than the real shape of things. I hardly see an object, but merely notice what class it belongs to—what ticket I ought to apply to it.

18. Everybody is familiar with the fact that the ordinary man does not see things as they are, but only sees certain *fixed types*. To begin with, we see separate things with distinct outlines where as a matter of fact we know that what exists is merely a continuous gradation of colour. Then even in outline itself we are unable to perceive the individual. We have in our minds certain fixed conceptions about the shape of a leg. Mr Walter Sickert is in the habit of telling his pupils that they are unable to draw any individual arm because they think of it as an arm ; and because they think of it as an arm they think they know what it ought to be. If it were a piece of almond rock you could draw it, because you have no preconceived notions as to the way the almonds should come. As a rule, then, we never ever perceive the real shape and individuality of objects. We only see stock types. We tend to see not *the* table but only *a* table.

19. One can sum up the whole thing by a metaphor which must not, however, be taken too literally. Suppose that the various kinds of emotions and other things which one wants to represent are represented by various curved lines. There are in reality an infinite number of these curves all differing slightly from

each other. But language does not and could not take account of all these curves. What it does do is to provide you with a certain number of standard types by which you can roughly indicate the different classes into which the curves fall. It is something like the wooden curves which architects employ — circles, ellipses, and so forth—by suitable combinations of which they can draw approximately any curve they want, but only approximately. So with ordinary language. Like the architect's curves it only enables us to describe approximately. Now the artist, I take it, is the person who in the first place is able to see an individual curve. This vision he has of the individuality of the curve breeds in him a dissatisfaction with the conventional means of expression which allow all its individualities to escape.

20. The artist has a double difficulty to overcome. He has in the first place to be a person who is emancipated from the very strong habits of the mind which make us see not individual things but stock types. His second difficulty comes when he tries to express the individual thing which he has seen. He finds then that not only has his mind habits, but that language, or whatever medium of expression he employs, also has its fixed ways. It is only by a certain tension of mind that he is able to force the mechanism of expression out of the way in which it tends to go and into the way he wants. To vary slightly

my metaphor of the curves. Suppose that in order to draw a certain individual curve which we perceive, you are given a piece of bent steel spring which has a natural curvature of its own. To make that fit the curve you want you will have to press it to that curve along the whole of its length with all your fingers. If you are unable to keep up this pressure and at one end slacken the pressure, then at that end you will not get the curve you were trying to draw, but the rounded-off curve of the spring itself.

You can observe this actual process at work in all the different arts. You may suppose that in music, for example, a man trying to express and develop a certain theme in the individual form in which it appeared to him might, if he relaxed his grip over the thing, find that it had a tendency to slacken off into resemblances to already heard things. This comparison also illustrates what happens in the decay of any art. Original sincerity, which is often almost grotesque in its individuality, slackens off in the rounded curves of "prettiness."

21. The psychology of the process is something of this kind. You start off with some actual and vividly felt experience. It may be something seen or something felt. You find that when you have expressed this in straightforward language that you have not expressed it at all. You have only expressed it approximately. All the individuality of the emotion

as you experienced it has been left out. The straightforward use of words always lets the individuality of things escape. Language, being a communal apparatus, only conveys over that part of the emotion which is common to all of us. If you are able to observe the actual individuality of the emotion you experience, you become dissatisfied with language. You persist in an endeavour to so state things that the meaning does not escape, but is definitely forced on the attention of the reader. To do this you are compelled to invent new metaphors and new epithets. It is here, of course, that the popular misunderstanding about originality comes in. It is usually understood by the outsider in the arts that originality is a desirable quality in itself. Nothing of the kind. It is only the defects of language that make originality necessary. It is because language will not carry over the exact thing you want to say, that you are compelled simply, in order to be accurate, to invent original ways of stating things.

22. The motive power behind any art is a certain freshness of experience which breeds dissatisfaction with the conventional ways of expression because they leave out the individual quality of this freshness. You are driven to new means of expression because you persist in an endeavour to get it out exactly as you felt it.

You could define art, then, as a passionate desire for accuracy, and the essentially æsthetic emotion as the excitement which is generated by direct communication. Ordinary language communicates nothing of the individuality and freshness of things. As far as that quality goes we live separated from each other. The excitement of art comes from this rare and unique communication.

23. Creation of imagery is needed to force language to convey over this *freshness* of impression. The particular kind of art we are concerned with here, at any rate, can be defined as an attempt to convey over something which ordinary language and ordinary expression lets slip through. The emotion conveyed by an art in this case, then, is the exhilaration produced by the direct and unusual communication of this fresh impression. To take an example : What is the source of the kind of pleasure which is given to us by the stanza from Keats' " Pot of Basil," which contains the line

" And she forgot the blue above the trees " ?

I do not put forward the explanation I give here as being, as a matter of fact, the right one, for Keats might have had to put trees for the sake of the rhyme, but I suppose for the sake of illustration that he was free to put what he liked. Why then did he put " blue above the trees " and not " sky " ? " Sky " is just as attractive an expression. Simply for this reason, that he instinctively felt that the word " sky " would not convey over the actual vividness and the actuality of the feeling he wanted to express. The choice of the right detail, the blue above the trees, forces that vividness on you and is the cause of the kind of thrill it gives you.

24. This particular argument is concerned only with a very small part of the effects which can be produced by poetry, but I have only used it as an illustration. I am not trying to explain poetry, but only to find out in a very narrow field of art, that of the use of imagery, what exactly the kind of emotion you call æsthetic consists of. The element in it which will be found in the rest of art is not the accidental fact that imagery conveys over an actually felt visual sensation, but the actual character of that communication, the fact that it hands you over the sensation as directly as possible, attempts to get it over bodily with all the qualities it possessed for you when you experienced it.

The feeling conveyed over to one is almost a kind of instinctive feeling. You get continuously from good imagery this conviction that the poet is constantly in presence of a vividly felt physical and visual scene.

25. You can perhaps trace this out a little more clearly in a wider art, that of prose description, the depicting of a character or emotion. You are not concerned here with handing over any visual scene, but in an attempt to get an emotion as near as possible as you feel it. You find that language has the same defects as the metaphors we have just

been talking about. It lets what you want to say escape. Each of us has his own way of feeling, liking and disliking. But language denotes these states by the same word in every case, so that it is only able to fix the objective and impersonal aspect of the emotions which we feel. Language, as in the first case, lets what you want to say slip through. In any writing which you recognise as good there is always an attempt to avoid this defect of language. There is an attempt, by the adding of certain kinds of intimate detail, to lift the emotion out of the impersonal and colourless level, and to give to it a little of the individuality which it really possesses.

26. Certain kinds of prose, at any rate, never attempt to give you any visual presentment of an object. To do so would be quite foreign to its purpose. It is endeavouring always not to give you any image, but to hurry you along to a conclusion. As in algebra certain concrete things are embodied in signs or counters which are moved about according to rule without being visualised at all in the process, so certain type situations and arrangements of words move automatically into certain other arrangements without any necessity at all to translate the words back into concrete imagery. In fact, any necessity to visualise the words you are using would be an impediment, it would delay the process of reasoning. When the words are merely counters they can be moved about much more rapidly.

Now any tendency towards counter language of this kind has to be carefully avoided by poetry. It always endeavours, on the contrary, to arrest you and to make you continuously see a physical thing.

27. Language, we have said, only expresses the lowest common denominator of the emotions of one kind. It leaves out all the individuality of an emotion as it really exists and substitutes for it a kind of stock or type emotion. Now here comes the additional observation which I have to make. As we not only express ourselves in words, but for the most part think also in them, it comes about that not only do we not express more than the impersonal element of an emotion, but that we do not, as a matter of fact, perceive more. The average person as distinct from the artist does not even *perceive* the individuality of their own emotions. Our faculties of perception are, as it were, crystallised out into certain moulds. Most of us, then, never see things as they are, but see only the stock types which are embodied in language.

This enables one to give a first rough definition of the artist. It is not sufficient to say that an artist is a person who is able to convey over the actual things he sees or the emotions he feels. It is necessary before that that he should be a person who is able to emancipate himself from the moulds which language and ordinary perception force on him and be able to see things freshly as they really are.

166

Though one may have some difficulty at first sight in seeing that one only perceives one's own emotions in stock types, yet the thing is much more easy to observe in the actual perception of external things with which you are concerned in painting.

28. I exaggerate the place of imagery simply because I want to use it as an illustration.

In this case something is physically presented ; the important thing is, of course, not the fact of the visual representation, but the communication over of the actual contact with reality.

It is because he realises the inadequacy of the usual that he is obliged to invent.

The gradual conclusion of the whole matter (and only as a conclusion) is that language puts things in a stereotyped form.

This is not the only kind of effect produced on one by verse but it is (if one extends the same quality to the other aspects of verse I have left out) the one essentially æsthetic emotion it produces on us. Readers of poetry may attach more importance to the other things, but this is the quality the poets recognise among each other. If one wants to fix it down then one can describe it as a " kind of instinctive feeling which is conveyed over to one, that the poet is describing something which is actually present to him, which he realises visually at first hand."

Is there anything corresponding to this in Painting ?

29. The essential element in the pleasure given us by a work of art lies in the feeling given us by this rare accomplishment of *direct communication*. Mr Berenson in his book on the Florentine painters expresses in a different vocabulary what is essentially the same feeling. The part of the book I am thinking of is that where he explains the superiority of Giotto to Duccio. He picks out the essential quality of a painting as its *life-communicating* quality, as rendered by form and movement. Form in the figure arts gives us pleasure because it has extracted and presented to us the structural significance of objects more completely than we (unless we be also great artists) could have grasped them by ourselves. By emphasis the artist gives us an intimate realisation of an object. In ordinary life I realise a given object, say with the given intensity *two*. An artist realises this with the intensity *four* and by his manner of emphasising it makes me realise it with the same intensity. This exhilarates me by communicating a sense of increased capacity. In that sense it may be said to be life-communicating. This emphasis can be conveyed in various ways : by form as in Giotto, and by movement expressed in line, as in Botticelli. This is exactly what Bergson is getting at. But instead of saying that an artist makes you realise with intensity *four* what you previously realised with intensity *two*, he would say that he makes you realise something

which you actually did not perceive before. When you come to the detailed application of this to art you find that they are both different ways of saying the same thing. They both agree in picking out this life-communicating quality as the essentially æsthetic one. And they both give the same analysis of the feat accomplished by the artist. The advantage of Bergson's account of the matter is that the expressions he uses are part of a definite conception of reality and not mere metaphors invented specially for the purpose of describing art. More than that, he is able to explain why it is that the ordinary man does not perceive things at all *vividly* and can only be made to do so by the artist. Both these things are of very little advantage as far as actual art criticism is concerned, but they are distinct advantages to anyone who wants to place art definitely in relation to other human activities.

THE PHILOSOPHY OF
INTENSIVE MANIFOLDS

THE PHILOSOPHY OF INTENSIVE
MANIFOLDS

IF one wanted to give the broadest possible description of the aim that Bergson pursues in all his work one would have to say that it was an endeavour to prove that we arrive at a certain picture of the nature of reality, not because such is, as a matter of fact, the nature of things, but because a certain inveterate tendency of the mind distorts things in that direction. That is giving the broadest possible statement of it ; the nature and importance of the effort becomes clearer when you state it in particular instead of general terms. The habit of mind which he thinks distorts instead of revealing is simply the ordinary use of the logical intellect. The theory to which we are led is that which considers the world as being in reality a vast machine. Huxley called it the nightmare of determinism—a nightmare most conveniently described by a quotation from a book of Münsterberg's :—

" Science is to me not a mass of disconnected information, but the certainty that there is no change in the universe, no

173

motion of an atom, and no sensation of a consciousness which does not come and go absolutely in accordance with natural laws ; the certainty that nothing can exist outside the gigantic mechanism of causes and effects ; necessity moves the stars in the sky and necessity moves the emotions in my mind."

The fact that Bergson does deal successfully with this nightmare seems to me to constitute his principal achievement. It forms the background which makes him appear so significant.

To repeat again, then, the general idea behind Bergson's work : It is an endeavour to prove that we seem inevitably to arrive at the mechanistic theory simply because the intellect, in dealing with a certain aspect of reality, distorts it in that direction. It can deal with matter but it is absolutely incapable of understanding life. In explaining vital phenomena it only distorts them, in exhibiting them as very complex mechanical phenomena. To obtain a complete picture of reality it is necessary to employ another faculty of the mind, which, after defining it, Bergson calls intuition. It is useless then to dream of one science of nature, for there must be two—one dealing with matter which will be built up by the intellect, and the other dealing with certain aspects of life which will employ intuition.

The idea that there are two methods of

thinking, the rational or mechanical on the one hand, and on the other hand the vital and more instinctive, is of course an idea which has been familiar for a long time outside philosophy. It occurs, for example, in Burke's writings on social and political matters.

What Bergson has done is to analyse out accurately and exactly the nature of this difference, and it is precisely in this accurate analysis of the difference between the two contrasted ways of looking at things that you get the essence of his philosophy. It seems to me then to be absolutely useless in explaining him to give anything else but the precise and accurate statement of his conception of the difference. It is no use generalising it. It is no use saying that he thinks the logical intellect is unable to grasp the essence of life, and that reality flows through the meshes of the net set for it by reason. Such statements do represent what he says, but they represent it so loosely that the whole importance of what he is getting at slips through. If you are firmly convinced that the mechanistic theory is the true account of the world, you are not in the least likely to be shifted from your view by vague statements of that kind.

It is necessary then to show exactly in what way Bergson thinks that our ordinary methods of explanation distort reality. The process of explanation itself is generally quite an unconscious one. We explain things and it never strikes us to consider what it is we have done. We are as it were *inside* the process and we cannot observe it, but you may get a hint of its nature by observing its effects. In any explanation you start off with certain phenomena, and you transform them into something else and say : " This is what really happens." There is something about this second state that satisfies the demands of your intellect, which makes you say : " This is perfectly clear." You have in your mind a model of what is clear and comprehensible, and the process of explanation consists in expressing all the phenomena of nature in the terms of this model. I ought to say here that I am speaking not of ordinary explanation, but of explanation when it has gone to its greatest lengths, which is when it has worked itself out in any completed science like mechanics.

As an example of the kind of thing which the intellect does consider perfectly clear and comprehensible you can think of a lot of pieces on a draught board. When you are told where the pieces are, and what moves they make, then the mind is satisfied that it completely understands the phenomena. An omniscient intelligence could know no more about that board than you do. You find as a matter of fact that any science, as it tends towards perfection, tends to present reality as consisting of something exactly similar to this draught board. They all resolve the complex phenomena of nature into fixed separate elements changing only in position. They all adopt atomic theories, and the model of all the sciences is astronomy. In order to get a convenient nomenclature one calls all complex things which can be resolved into separate elements or atoms in this way " extensive manifolds."

It is suggested that this surprising unanimity in the results of the different sciences is not due to the nature of the phenomena they investigate, but rather to the nature of the instrument we use in explanation. We find atoms everywhere. We reduce everything to extensive manifolds. We always pursue the method of analysis simply because that is the only way in which the intellect can deal with things.

The question arises : Why is the intellect satisfied in this way ? The answer to this is quite simple and can be got from the etymology of the words which indicate explanation. Explanation means *ex plane*, that is to say, the opening out of things on a plain surface. There is the phrase, *the chestnut explains its leaves*, *i.e.* unfolds them. Then the French word is expliquer (explico) to unfold. The process of explanation is always a process of unfolding. A tangled mass is unfolded flat so that you can see all its parts separated out, and any tangle which can be separated out in this way must be of course an extensive manifold.

It seems then that the intellect distorts reality (if it does distort it) because it persists in unfolding things out in space. It is not satisfied unless it can see every part. It wants to form a picture. It is possible then that there may be a method of knowledge which refrains from forming pictures. Put in Bergson's words in the preface to his first book, which really contains in embryo the whole of everything he has ever done, " We think in terms of space—the insurmountable difficulties presented by certain philosophic problems arise from the fact that we separate out in space, phenomena which do not occupy space."

You might dimly suspect that there are other methods of knowledge besides that of analysis. I may have a perfect knowledge of a friend's face, *e.g.*, without being able to analyse it into parts. You may suspect that they are unanalysable. An expert can give a judgment on a picture, a judge on a complex case, without being able to give any reasons for their judgment, that is without being able to analyse out the element which was responsible for it. Anyone can add to this list indefinitely. In fact all of us are prepared to agree that at any rate such things as *apparent* intuitions exist. But if we have been sufficiently disciplined in science we refuse to admit that these are real intuitions or that there is any other method of knowledge which is different to the ordinary straightforward one. We say that the mind has unconsciously analysed and so arrived at its conclusions. We refuse to admit that things exist which can't be analysed. Life, we persist in thinking, appears to be un-analysable merely because it is so extremely complex. In the end we shall be able to analyse it. So with all these appearances of intuitive knowledge, they are really only complex examples of ordinary knowledge.

Now, as in the case of the intellect, it is necessary to make these things much more precise before it can be got at. I shall endeavour to show that intuition can be defined as the method of knowledge by which we seize an intensive manifold, a thing absolutely unseizable by the intellect.

Explanation is an endeavour to make things comprehensible. It is suggested that we have too narrow a standard of what is compre-hensible and clear. Bergson is endeavouring to widen this standard, to make it more elastic, to provide an alternative model. It is be-cause of the narrowness of our conception of what is clear that we are driven into so many difficulties. We feel convinced for quite other reasons that certain things exist which cannot be reduced to mechanical or spacial terms. As we have such a narrow standard of what is clear we can't fit them into any natural explanation, the result is that we have to give extremely unnatural explanations of them. We have to say that these things are

Inconceivable and Inexpressible, both with capital I's. For example, as Free-will will not fit into the mechanical conception of things, and we are at the same time convinced that it exists, we have to find a place for it in a world of things in themselves. The result is that a certain condition of strain is set up. Bergson attempts to ease this strain and to let these things come back to the ordinary world by altering the standard of clear explanation. He endeavours to show that certain finite things, while quite incomprehensible by our ordinary standards, yet exist.

What exactly are these things ? You will remember that the intellect which always thinks, as it were, in space, which always insists on having a clear diagram or picture, insists on analysing complex things into an aggregate of separate elements which we called extensive manifolds. In order that the intellect may be able to completely grasp reality, it is necessary that reality should be composed entirely in this way. Suppose, however, that there existed in nature certain finite things whose parts interpenetrated in such a manner that they could not be separated or analysed out. The intellect would then be unable to understand the nature of these things, for it persists in forming a diagram, and in a diagram each part is separated from every other part. It is difficult to give an idea of what one means by an interpenetration of parts which cannot be separated. One naturally supposes that what is meant here is an extraordinary inexplicable tangle which can't be unravelled. But that would not be at all what was intended for here one can't separate the parts because they are mixed in such an extraordinary complex way. In theory, at any rate, one could separate them out. One is to suppose rather an absolute interpenetration—a complex thing which yet cannot be said to have parts because the parts run into each other, forming a continuous whole, and whose parts cannot even be conceived as existing separately. It has differences, but these differences could not be numbered. It could not therefore be called a quantitative multiplicity, but a qualitative one. For the sake of convenience and the contrast with the other thing I prefer to call it an intensive manifold.

I don't suppose that I have succeeded in conveying a very clear idea of what an intensive manifold is, or would be, because by its very nature, one's intellect, as it were, wriggles away from the idea. One's ordinary intellectual imagination which persists in making spacial pictures of things naturally finds it inconceivable to imagine a thing which couldn't possibly exist in space.

One can illustrate the difficulty that one has in conceiving it by thinking of one epithet I have used to describe it, namely interpenetration.

You cannot even form a picture of the kind

of interpenetration you mean. If you melt salt in water, after a time salt would be found in every particle of the water, and you might think then that here you had interpenetration. But no : your mind cannot support an idea of that kind. It sets to work and imagines that the molecules of salt fit in between the molecules of water. It so gets rid of the idea interpenetration and reduces everything to an extensive manifold. In this little instance it might be argued that there is no distortion. But if you suppose that there do exist in the world some instances of real interpenetration, then the intellect, working by analysis, would be incapable of understanding them.

All this is mere supposition. If such intensive manifolds exist, if there are cases of real interpenetration, then Bergson will have proved his point, namely, that the intellect cannot deal with the whole of reality, that there cannot be merely one science, and that completely to understand the nature of reality some other faculty of the mind, some second method of cognition, must be employed.

Two questions, then, have to be considered at this point :—

(1) Is there such a faculty as intuition, as distinct from the intellect, which enables one to know certain things without being able to analyse or to state them ?

(2) Are there as a matter of fact existing in nature any such things as intensive manifolds ?

This is the crucial point in Bergson's reasoning, the point at which it passes from mere supposition to fact.

It was suggested that the view of the world as a mechanism was due, not to the nature of reality itself, but to certain preferences of the intellect. That the intellect in fact distorts reality. It distorts it for this reason, that in explaining things it always insists on unfolding them into parts, or analysing them.

It was pointed out that if the intellect came across an intensive manifold—that is a finite thing—of such a nature that its parts interpenetrate and cannot be separated out, that it would endeavour in roundabout ways to replace them by complicated extensives, and so would distort reality.

But that remains pure theory, and no real step towards an attack on mechanism has been made until you have definitely proved the existence of such an intensive manifold.

If you can prove that even one of them exists then you have got the fulcrum with which you can begin to shift mechanism. You must find a concrete example ; otherwise the thing remains entirely in the air.

The particular part of reality in which Bergson first attempted to prove the existence of interpenetration was that of our own mental life. This is the part of reality in which we may be supposed to get at the nature of things most intimately and which may give the key to the rest. This is the subject of Bergson's first book, *Time and Free-will*.

At first sight, mental life, like things in the physical world, does appear to be resolvable into separate elements. It does appear to form really an extensive manifold, and not an intensive one, as Bergson claims. You are able to describe what you feel, and no description is, of course, possible without analysis. I can say I feel annoyed, or that I was prompted to a certain action by a certain motive, or that I had such and such a sequence of ideas. You do appear to be able to form a picture of the mind then as composed of a succession of clearly outlined states following one another. If that were correct it could be dealt with by a science of exactly the same character as that constituted by the physical sciences. There is nothing here which the intellect cannot deal with ; there is no necessity for any different way of knowing things.

But it is not difficult to see that such a description of the nature of the mind is a very superficial one. There are *no* clearly outlined and separated states ; in fact there are no separate states of mind at all : each state fades away into and interpenetrates the next state. The whole thing being continuous, then consider any description such as " He felt annoyed." This is in no sense an accurate description of a man's actual state of mind. The feeling of " annoyance " as it occurs to any one person is perfectly individual, and is coloured by his whole personality. Language, however, has to use, to describe this particular state of "annoyance," the same word in every case, and is thus only able to fix the objective and impersonal aspect of the emotion. Every emotion is composed of a thousand different elements which dissolve into and permeate each other without any precise outline. In this lies the individuality of the emotion. As soon as you begin to analyse and to attempt to describe it in words you take away from it all the individuality which the emotion possesses as occurring in a certain person.

To describe accurately, then, any emotion —to give it accurately and not approximately —you would have to describe at the same time the whole personality in which it occurs, which is only another way of saying that mental life forms a whole which cannot be analysed into parts.

But the fact remains that superficially you can, as a matter of fact, analyse and describe the flow of mental life. How is this ?

The fact that certain parts of the mind can be separated into elements is not due entirely to the nature of the intellect. The intellect, it is true, always insists on analysing things into elements, but it would not meet here with the success it does did it not correspond with something actual in the nature of the mind itself.

Bergson explains this by his theory of the

two selves. Fundamentally, the mind is a flux of interpenetrating elements which cannot be analysed out. But on the surface this living self gets covered over with a crust of clean cut psychic states which are separated one from the other and which can be analysed and described. This crystallisation into separate states has come about mainly for the purposes of action and communication in social life. If each new idea gradually permeated the whole like a drop of water does a pool, then decision and action would be slow and ineffective. So for purposes of communication, you must be able to describe, and to do that you must have some stable crystallised-out states which you can talk about.

You thus have two different selves at two different levels. The superficial one which is the one usually perceived, and which comes into play at the ordinary level of daily life where each state can be separated out from each other state, and which so can be thoroughly understood by the ordinary intellect, and the more fundamental self which is only reached at certain moments of tension where all the states interpenetrate, and of which, it being an intensive manifold, no picture or description can be given.

For the purposes of a short exposition of Bergson it is inconvenient that it is so difficult to convey what he means by this fundamental self, because it is on the experiencing of this state that depends also what he means by an intuition. I said earlier that an intuition was the process of mind by which one obtained knowledge of an intensive manifold.

Obviously you can't understand, or be said to know in any way, an intensive manifold by means of the logical intellect because by the very nature of the thing you can't analyse it, and it is so indescribable. But although indescribable it is not unknowable, for Bergson supposes that in an intuition you have complete knowledge of these things. You have a complete and complex state of knowledge, of a complex thing, containing differences within it although these differences are not separable and can't be unfolded out. The simplest way of describing it would be to say that you had a complex feeling about the matter, were not " feeling " such a dangerous word to use in this connection.

But all this has rather the appearance of a kind of abstract miracle and an elaborately built-up piece of abstraction which corresponds to no real process. You can only fill it in with the details that make it actual and real by the experiences drawn from the mental phenomena which Bergson calls the fundamental self.

In a moment of tension, when a man is moving on the level of the fundamental self, he will have a knowledge of what is happening in him which is of a fundamentally different character to the ordinary kind of knowledge. What that difference is can only be got at by crude metaphor. If you think of mental life as a flowing stream, then ordinary intellectual knowledge is like looking at that stream from the outside : you get a clear and perfectly describable picture. Imagine now that you are turned into a cross section of this flowing stream, that you have no sense of sight, that in fact your only sense is a sense of pressure. Then although you will have no clear picture or representation of the stream at all, you will in spite of that have a complete knowledge of it as a complex sense of the varying directions of the forces pressing on you. If you put yourself in this position with regard to your own inner life—and this is what Bergson means by an intuition—then you will realise that it is composed not of separate things but of interpenetrating tendencies. It is always a process which contains differences implicitly and not separated out. It is composed of a million different elements which at the same time are not elements at all, because they melt into one another with not the least tendency to be separated one from the other. Such a state can be directly experienced, and yet is a state which is absolutely inconceivable intellectually, simply because it can't be analysed.

But it is extremely important here to notice that there is nothing mysterious either about the state of mind or about the method of cognition by which you become aware of it. There is nothing infinite or ineffable about the fundamental self. It is a perfectly finite thing and at the same time there is nothing miraculous about one's intuition of it. And it is just at this point that a good deal of academic criticism of Bergson seems to me to go wrong. Because the process of intuition is by its nature an indescribable process, it seems to be assumed that it is not a part of normal experience. The critics then pass on to the statement that as, in Bergson's view, certain aspects of reality cannot be seized by the intellect but only by some mysterious faculty of the mind, that therefore his system is only a kind of subtly disguised agnosticism.

This seems to me to be an entirely wrong view. What Bergson means by an intuition is a perfectly normal and frequent phenomenon. It seems a curious thing to say, but in all probability any literary man or artist would understand—would grasp much more easily—what Bergson means by an intuition. It is a process with which they are perfectly familiar and which isn't in the least mysterious to them. Nearly all of them constantly exercise the faculty. "Anyone who has attempted any literary composition, for example, knows that when the subject has been thoroughly studied and all the notes collected, it is necessary, before one begins the work of composition itself, to make sometimes a difficult effort to place oneself as it were at the heart of the subject."* In this state of tension one receives an impulsion, a sense of

* Bergson : *Introduction to Metaphysics.*

direction, which, when it develops itself as it goes along, picks up and makes use of all the notes that have been made before. The point to notice here is that at the beginning of this act, at this moment of tension, all the separate parts which before and after were separated out, were gathered up together in this act of intuition. They didn't exist side by side in the mind as they would have done in any intellectual representation. In Coleridge's phrase, they were fused together in the central heat of the imagination.

In terms of this conception of the two layers of mental life, the superficial and the fundamental self, I can state very briefly Bergson's conception of Free-will. He thinks that on the level of the superficial self our actions are to a great extent quite determined and automatic. One clear cut psychic state influences the next, just as, mechanically, one body influences another in the physical way. In this state the real flux of our feelings isn't concerned at all. For example, when the alarum clock strikes in the morning, the impression does not as a rule disturb the whole consciousness like a stone falling into a pool of water, but merely stirs an idea solidified on the surface, the idea of getting up. The two ideas both solidified, as it were, on the top of the mind have in the end become tied up with one another, so that one follows the other without the deeper self being at all involved. The majority of our daily acts are performed in this way and it is greatly to one's advantage that such is the case.

But there are acts of a different kind to this when the outer crust gets broken by the inner self breaking through at a moment of tension and you get what may be called a free act. Such acts are of rare occurrence. It is only at moments of tension and crisis that we choose in defiance of what is generally called a motive. Thus understood our free acts are exceptional.

This theory of the difference between the two kinds of manifold, the intensive and the extensive, and the two kinds of knowledge by which they can be dealt with, intellect and intuition, constitutes only one half of Bergson's system. Parallel with this method, with this alteration of the tools with which we are to work, should go an account of the new theory of the nature of reality which the use of these new tools produces, which is involved in Bergson's conception of *Change and Time*.

To get at Bergson's conception of Change you have to remember his main point (that the intellect distorts things by insisting on one method of explanation) and turning to this particular question, try and find out whether one's difficulties are not due to some distortion of the real nature of Change produced in this way.

How does the intellect deal with Change? As we have seen it tries to make out that all bodies can be analysed out into separable elements, so that it has consequentially to reduce all change to a mere change in position of these particles. In fact it explains change by denying its existence.

One can get a picture of the type in terms of which the mind insists on conceiving change by thinking of the motion of billiard balls on an ideally smooth table where there is no friction. It would be impossible here to discover and conceive the existence of freedom. There is in fact no change at all. You can predict with certainty the position of the balls at any future moment, for you have a fixed number of elements moving under fixed laws.

But—and here comes one of the most important elements for the understanding of what Bergson is getting at—this is only a true account of change if you admit that everything can in reality be analysed into separate elements like the balls on the table. If it can, then the future must be determined ; but we have just seen that mental life at the level of the fundamental self cannot. It is an interpenetrating whole : it is not composed of elements. It changes, but the way in which it changes will not fit into the kind of conception which the intellect forms of change.

If we suppose that free acts are possible we are landed : it follows that real novelty is possible ; that things can happen which could not have been foreseen even by an infinite intelligence. It seems difficult to believe that not only is the future unknown to us, but that it is at the present moment undecided. We admit chance relatively to our limited knowledge but we find it inconceivable that there is an element of absolute chance in the world. Our mind persists in thinking that if we only knew all the laws which govern things we could predict the future. If I picture my motion through time as being like motion along a country road, then I am quite prepared to admit that owing to my vision being limited by the size of the hedges I cannot see the course of the road ahead of me. But I am firmly convinced that the road ahead of me does exist all the time in a fixed direction, and that if I had absolute knowledge—if I could take a bird's-eye-view—I should be able to see it.

We find ourselves unable to rid ourselves of this idea. Freedom is inconceivable and this is the greatest argument as a matter of fact for determinism. The use of the word inconceivable suggests that here again you may have a difficulty caused solely by the intellect's persistence in explaining things in a certain fixed way.

The distortion that the intellect here produces is in our conception of the nature of change. It conceives change in such a way that the future seems always determined.

The inconceivability of an undetermined future does not in reality apply to it, for that inconceivability is only presented to the mind when it thinks of the changing phenomena as being composed of separated elements. It is possible to see then how, at this depth of mental life, where all the elements interpenetrate, and which so constitutes an intensive manifold, you may conceive the possibility of acts which could not have been predicted even by an absolute intelligence, and which were really creative acts.

With these two models of the kind of possible change one may more easily grasp what Bergson means by his doctrine of real time.

In the case where you have a number of elements merely changing in position, time is not really involved at all, for time makes no difference to them. They never alter ; they never grow old. At the end of years they may return to the same position as that from which they started.

More than that, if you doubled the speed at which the change of positions took place it would make no difference at all to the system. Take any example of such a system, say the astronomical one. The planets following certain fixed laws follow certain fixed courses. It would make absolutely no difference to those courses if you supposed the speed doubled.

In the first kind of change, where you merely get a rearrangement of parts, time makes no difference at all. You can imagine the process twice as fast without any alteration being produced in the process. In any case nothing really new can be produced.

But in the case of the second kind of change —that which you get at a deeper level—this is by no means true. Time does make a difference. Here you have no mere rearrangement of parts, but a continuous and real change resulting in the production of absolutely new and unpredictable states. It is this kind of change that Bergson calls *real* duration, or real time.

One could get a gross kind of metaphor for the difference between these two kinds of time in this way: If you conceive a perfectly smooth machine working in air you could not double the speed without altering the resistance of the air. But if you had a perfectly smooth machine working in a vacuum then you could make the speed what you liked without any difficulty. Now if the air here is supposed to represent time, then you see that ordinary mechanism as conceived by the intellect does not exist in time at all, for time makes no difference to it.

But you cannot alter the speed of mental life in the same way. In the mechanical world, then, time might flow with infinite rapidity and the entire past, present and future be spread out all at once. But inside us it is very different. In us time is undeniable fact. If I want to mix a glass of sugar and water I have to wait willy-nilly until the sugar melts. This is *real time ;* it coincides with my impatience, that is with a certain portion of my duration which I cannot contract as I like.

One could express the same idea in a different way, which brings out better the causes of it and the more important consequences of it. If a child has to fit together a jig-saw puzzle, it can learn to do it quicker and quicker. Theoretically indeed it requires no time to do it, because the result is already given. The picture is already created and the work of recomposing it can be supposed going faster and faster up to the point of being instantaneous. But to the artist who creates a picture, time is no longer an interval that can be lengthened or shortened. To contract it would be to modify the invention itself. The time taken up by the invention is one with the invention itself. It is the actual living progress of the thought, a kind of vital process like *ripening*.

Now here you get at the essence of the thing. *Real duration, real time* is an absolute thing which cannot be contracted or hastened because in it *real work* is being done, really new things are appearing.

In the world of mechanism, as you have seen, there is no real creation of new things, there is merely a rearrangement of fixed elements in various positions. They can't be said to exist in time, because nothing *new* happens, there is no *real time* because there is no *real change*. At a certain depth of mental life you experience real time because there is a real change ; new things are produced and not a mere rearranging of old parts. Time then is creation. In real time you get real creation and so real freedom.

The importance of all this is that it is in terms of the nature of mental life that we hope to find the key to reality. If this turns out to be true, then you will form a conception of the world very different from the mechanistic one. One must think of it as duration, that is to say, continuous growth in creation. A becoming never the same, never repeating itself, but always producing novelty, continually ripening and creating. Corresponding to the two methods of explanation—that by intensives and that by extensives—you have then two conceptions of reality as existing in space and in duration.

It is important to see that the inability under which we suffer, of being unable to conceive the existence of a real change in which absolutely new and unpredictable things can happen, is entirely due to that fixed habit of the intellect which insists that we shall analyse things into elements, and insists on that because it will have a picture in spatial terms.

Real change does exist but we shall always find it inconceivable if we try to form a picture of what we mean. When we think in that way we shall always reduce real change to the kind of change that you get in any mechanical system.

197

This then is the point reached in the argument at the present minute—

I started off with Bergson's method. The first application of this to reality resulted in the conception of the self I have just outlined. You find that in this case the mechanistic theory does not hold, and that fundamentally mind is a free creative activity.

But so far you have not moved outside the limits of the individual mind. As far as that is concerned one may be said to have refuted mechanism. But the retort is still open that the whole thing is subjective. It may be a kind of self delusion. Outside you the world of matter might still be considered as a mechanism.

You now get the second passage to reality in a deeper application of the method. You have still got to prove that this state of flux— this feeling of a free activity which you feel in a certain state of tension—is not merely a subjective state of mind, but does give you real information about a reality which exists outside you.

The first involves the relation of the mind and the body, and to this Bergson devoted his second book *Matter and Memory*.

The novelty of his treatment of this question is that he attempts to deal with it not as a mere matter of speculation, but on a basis provided by an examination of a body of empirical observations. He asserts that the theory he puts forward is the right one because it is the only one which satisfactorily accounts for these facts.

The only body of facts which we actually know in connection with the relation of mind and body are those connected with aphasia, *i.e.* the various ways in which we lose our memory for words.

Bergson's own account of the phenomena is this : What exactly happens when I bring to consciousness the picture of something that I saw yesterday ? We can understand it best by thinking of the process of becoming conscious or aware of the existence of an ordinary physical object.

I am not conscious of the existence of the table in the next room. Even if the table is brought into this room I shall not know that it exists until I have opened my eyes—that is until the table has managed to produce certain disturbances in the nerves which lead from my eyes to my brain. It is as if my brain were a keyboard and I only became conscious of the existence of things when they played on that keyboard.

Now apply this to the similar case of memory. Just as many things exist in the next room, of whose existence I am not conscious at this minute, so there exist trailed behind in me, as it were, a whole host of memories of my past of which I am at the present moment quite unconscious.

It is then as if all our memories existed quietly in a kind of next room where one was not conscious of their existence ; but that now and then one emerged and became actual by playing on the keyboard of that special part of the brain with which it was concerned.

What, then, should we see if we were able to look into the brain and to see all the atoms in motion ?

On the parallelist theory you would be able to tell everything that the person whose brain you were examining was thinking of.

If Bergson's account of the matter is the correct one, you would, when you looked into the brain, see only the parts of the whole thoughts of the man which had reached the stage when they were beginning to turn into, and to influence, action.

We should then know no more of what the man was thinking about than we should know about a play in a foreign tongue which we did not understand, from watching the movements of the actors.

That is, we should know only that part of his thoughts which involved action.

How much we shall learn from the movements of the actors will depend on the nature of the play—nearly everything if it is a pantomime, very little at all if it is a comedy. So with a man's brain. If he is pursuing a course of abstract reasoning we should be able to tell nothing at all from the state of his brain ; but if, on the contrary, his mind was occupied with a distinct visual image, or was just preparing to act, we should know nearly everything.

This theory cannot be understood unless one has grasped his idea of the intensives.

You may persist in asking the question : Where are these past memories stored ? The answer to that is that the whole of your past life is in the present. This inner stream which composes your inner self bears in it not the whole of your past in the form of completed pictures, but bears it in the form of potentiality. In this stream the elements are, as we have said, interpenetrated. All that happens in an act of recognition is that the interpenetrated parts get separated out.

The most familiar part of Bergson, which I can only state in a few sentences, comes in his account of evolution.

He holds that the only theory which will account for the fact of evolution is to suppose that it was produced by a kind of impulse which is something akin to the creative activity we find in our own mind, and which, inserted in matter, has gradually achieved the result which we now see.

This force or impulse is not a force in the ordinary sense of the term : it is not material at all. You cannot indeed give any representation of it at all for it is of the same nature as the kind of activity we find in ourselves, and which, being an intensive manifold, could not be understood by the intellect.

It is, I suppose, admitted as a fact that

there has been such a thing as a real evolution in time. You get on the surface of the earth an amazing variety of different kinds of life from the simple to the very complex. It is generally believed that the very complex forms are descended and have evolved from the more simple ones.

That is the fact with which we start. What kind of explanation has been given of it ?

There are two principal sets of theories about it which are known respectively as mechanism and finalism.

The first treats the whole of the phenomena of life and evolution as if they constituted merely an extraordinarily complicated kind of mechanism, and attempts to explain them in the same way as due to the action of the forces concerned. I have used the motion of billiard balls on an ideally smooth table as a convenient picture for any mechanistic system. I can use it again here. Suppose that you had a great number of balls on the table, all moving in various directions. Suppose that gradually, as a result solely of the forces exerted on them by their various collisions, they began to group themselves in large complex and fairly permanent arrangements. That represents the ordinary mechanistic conception of evolution. It represents exactly the kind of thing you get in Spencer, for example in his progress from homogeneity to heterogeneity. The important point about it is to see that the whole of the change has been produced solely as the result of the forces exerted upon the atoms. There is no plan or no desire to produce complexity.

. . . . In the finalistic conception life is supposed to be following a plan all laid down beforehand. It is supposed to be working towards some final end which is generally taken to be man.

Bergson's criticism of both these conceptions, mechanism and finalism, is that they both leave out duration altogether. Whether the complexity of life comes as the result of the working out of certain mechanical laws, or whether it is following a plan laid down for it, in both cases the future is fixed and could be known to an infinite intelligence. That is, they don't exist in real time at all—everything is *given*, there is no real creation. He asserts that the characteristic of all forms of life is that they emphatically exist in duration, *time* does make a difference to them. Time *bites* them and leaves the mark of his teeth on them. All living things grow old, whereas matter never does : it is always *constant* and always the *same*.

In life you do appear to get continuous evolution and creation. Bergson suggests then that the only theory which will fit the facts of evolution is to suppose that it is produced by a kind of *impulse* which is something akin to the creative activity we find in our own mind and which, inserted in matter, has, following out this creative activity, gradually achieved the result we see in evolution.

This impulse is not a force in the ordinary sense of the term ; it is not material at all. You cannot, indeed, give any representation of it, for it is of the same nature as the kind of activity we feel in ourselves and which being an intensive manifold could not be understood by the intellect. You are to conceive the original élan or impulse of life to be of the same nature as our own inner self. That is, it is an intensive manifold which contained many differences potentially and interpenetrated.

What *matter* does is to separate out distinctly into separate elements the characteristics which in the original impulse were interpenetrated. Evolution then is not a process of organisation, of building up, but one of dissociation.

It is this which gives Bergson the basis for an empirical proof for the *existence of this élan*.

There are of course two proofs, the direct one which comes from the intuition we have in ourselves of the existence of such an activity. But it is also possible to give a more empirical proof. On Bergson's hypothesis, we have seen, evolution is a separating out of elements which interpenetrated in the original impulse. If then you get the same organs developed on divergent lines of evolution, you have on Bergson's theory nothing to be surprised at, for they both develop it from their common origin ; but on the mechanistic theory, the thing will appear rather surprising.

Take a definite case. On two quite separate lines of evolution, that which includes the vertebrates and that which ends in the molluscs, you get an eye produced. Moreover this eye is composed of almost the same parts in both cases. Now on the mechanistic conception of evolution this phenomena is very difficult to account for.

In the first place, the eye is composed of a multitude of anatomical elements and tissues all of which are disposed with the greatest precision and harmony to serve the function of vision. That this precise and extremely complex arrangement of a vast multitude of parts, many of which are of highly specialised construction, should have been achieved by the accumulation of happy accidents is a sufficiently incredible supposition.

But another reason makes it more incredible still. An eye very similar in construction to our own is independently evolved in some species of mollusc. The mechanists are driven then to the supposition that the same kind of happy accident has occurred independently in two branches of the tree of life. It is as if two walkers starting from different points and wandering at random should not only meet but should throughout their walks have described two identical curves.

Does Bergson's hypothesis enable us to give a

better account of this phenomenon? In the first place he would say that we approach the question of explanation in the wrong way. The eye appears as an infinitely complicated structure. Any mechanical theory seeks to show how the infinite multiplicity of the parts has been added bit by bit. The whole process then becomes almost inconceivable. One cannot imagine however it has been accomplished. Bergson says that this difficulty is as usual entirely due to the intellect's persistence in analysing things. We persist in thinking that the eye must have been *constructed* just as we construct a house by adding piece to piece. Whereas if we could get at the act from inside we should find that it was a simple indivisible process. The life impulse finding itself opposed by matter makes an effort to overcome the obstacle and does this in a simple unanalysable act which results in the visual apparatus.

But as long as we try to reconstruct the process intellectually, we shall be landed in hopeless difficulty. The act of lifting my arm is a perfectly simple one to me. But it becomes hopelessly complicated when one attempts to analyse it out into all the molecular motions of the muscle of which it is composed.

We have compared the process with which nature constructs an eye to the simple act with which we raise the hand. To make it more accurate, suppose that the hand meets with some resistance—that it has to pass through iron filings that are compressed and offer resistance to it. At a certain moment the hand will have exhausted its effort and at this moment the filings will be massed and arranged in a certain definite form. So with the evolution of the eye. The farther the hand goes the greater the complexity of the massed filings ; and the farther the impulse in life has gone, the greater the complexity of the eye produced.

Now suppose that the hand and arm are *invisible*. Lookers-on would speculate as to the reason of the arrangement of the filings they see.

Some will account for the action of each filing by the action of the neighbouring filings. These are the *mechanists*. This is the kind of view you get in Spencer where the whole of evolution is supposed to follow from the various attractions of the atoms in the universe.

Others will prefer to think that a plan has presided over the details of these actions. These are the finalists.

But the truth is that there has been one indivisible act, that of the hand passing through the filings.

This is why you get similar eyes in divergent species, for the eye is not constructed by addition of parts, but springs from the same impulse present in every species, and springs from a common origin.

This enables one to see why it is that a similar kind of eye can be met with in two very widely removed animal species. If along both lines of evolution the progress towards vision has gone equally far, the visual organ will be the same in both cases, for the form of the organ merely expresses a measure in which the exercise of the function has been obtained.

It is easy then to see in what respect Bergson's view differs from the mechanistic one. That view of evolution considers that where you get a certain complex organism, owing to the action of natural forces you get a very complex organisation of matter ; that there you get life and consciousness. Bergson's own view is the exact contrary of this. The complex organisation does not produce, but is produced by, life.

The characteristic of matter is necessity. The characteristic of the impulse which has produced life is, on the contrary, a free creative activity. The process of evolution can only be described as the gradual insertion of more and more freedom into matter. The original impulse of life builds up certain very complex explosive kinds of compounds which enable it to bring a certain indetermination into matter. In the amœba, then, you might say that the impulse had manufactured a small leak through which free activity could be inserted into the world, and the progress of evolution has been the gradual enlargement of this leak. But, on the other hand, it is necessary to differentiate this view from finalism. On the surface it looks very like it. The gradual insertion of freedom into matter looks very like a plan laid down beforehand. But it is in reality quite different.

One can show in what exactly this difference consists, by showing the part that chance has played in evolution, and by explaining in what sense *Man* can be said to be the goal of the process.

As to the mechanism by which this has been accomplished. The brain of man looks very like the brain of some other animals. In what lies the difference ? It is this : That in the animals any motor mechanisms in the brain which correspond to habits have no other function than the accomplishment of the movements necessitated by those habits. But in man these habits can have a second result, and so by holding other motor habits in check, can overcome automatism and set consciousness free. It is just the difference between a mechanism which engages the attention and a mechanism from which it can be diverted. Bergson illustrates this difference by the following metaphor. The primitive steam-engine required the presence of a person exclusively employed to turn on and turn off taps, either to let steam into the cylinder or to throw cold spray into it. A boy employed on this work and who had got very tired of it got the idea of tying the handles of the taps with cords to the beam of the engine. Then

the machine opened and closed the taps itself. If you looked at the machine before and
after this alteration without taking any notice
of the boy, there would appear to be very
little difference in structure. But if you look
at the two boys, in the first case all his time
was taken up by watching and in the second
he was free to go and play as he chose. The
difference between the brain of a man and the
brain of an animal is probably of this kind.

You could describe the facts of evolution,
then, by saying that it seems as if an immense
current of consciousness had traversed matter,
endeavouring to organise this matter so that
it could introduce freedom into it.

But, in doing this, consciousness has itself
been ensnared in certain directions. Matter
has captured the consciousness which was
organising it and entrapped it in its own automatism. In the vegetable kingdom, for example, automatism and unconsciousness have
become the rule. In the animals consciousness has more success, but along the whole
course of evolution, liberty is dogged by automatism, and is in the long run stifled by it.
In man alone has it organised matter into any
effective freedom. One can get at a picture
of the course of evolution in this way : It
is as if a current of consciousness flowed down
into matter as into a tunnel, and, making
efforts to advance on every side, digs galleries,
most of which are stopped by a rock which is
too hard, but which in one direction at least

has broken through the rock and back into life again once more. This direction is the line of evolution resulting in man.

But if you accept this as a correct picture of the progress of evolution, the question naturally suggests itself to you : Why did this current of consciousness endeavour to assert itself in matter ? What possible object could it have ? Bergson suggests that an answer can be found to this question by considering the analogy of literary activity. You may start writing a poem in an endeavour to express a certain idea which is present in your mind in a very hazy shape. The effort to express that idea in verse, the struggle with language, forces the idea as it were back on itself and brings out the original idea in a clearer shape. Before it was only confused. The idea has grown and developed because of the obstacles it had to meet. It may be, then, that the function of matter in regard to consciousness is this : It is destined to bring to precision, in the form of distinct personalities, tendencies or potentialities which at first were mingled.

The passage through matter may give to a part of the current of consciousness a certain kind of coherence which enables it to survive as a permanent entity after its passage. And as it is only with man that consciousness has finally left the tunnel. Everywhere else it has remained in prison. And as every other species corresponds to the arrest of something which in man succeeds in over-coming resistance, so displaying itself in characters capable of remembering and of controlling their actions, we shall have no repugnance in admitting that in man, though perhaps in man alone, consciousness pursues its path beyond the bodily life.

The stage in the argument that has been reached at this point is this : You have proved that the inner self which you experi-ence in a moment of tension is not produced by the brain and is to a great extent indepen-dent of it. At such moments of tension, then, you reach a reality which passes outside your physical self. But that is not a satisfactory conclusion to the argument, for it leaves the thing rather suspended in the air. The further question is suggested : What is this duration apart from you ?

The principal object of Bergson's *Creative Evolution*, is to prove that this pure duration which we experience at the level of the deeper self is identical with the kind of current which runs through all life. In that way he rounds off his position. A certain dissatisfaction is left by the first book, *Time and Free-will*, because it is entirely subjective. It only concerns itself with the analysis of one's own mind. The second book, *Matter and Memory*, to a certain extent removes this, because it proves that in duration we have something independent of the body. A certain dis-satisfaction is still left, and this is removed by

Creative Evolution, which proves that this duration is identical with life.

In this latter book, then, he definitely sets his thought solidly on a fixed base. Once it is proved, nearly all the vagueness disappears from the terms which he uses. One has said vaguely that in an intuition you place yourself inside the object instead of surveying it from the outside. We are now able to give a definite meaning to that phrase. " To place yourself inside the object " is no longer a merely metaphorical expression. In that state of mind in which you feel and experience duration, and which we have called intuition, you are actually inside that stream of impulse which constitutes life. The difference, too, between intellect and intuition, which before one had merely taken as given, as an ultimate fact which one couldn't explain, one is able to a certain extent to show how it originated. One is able to deduce the characteristics of the intellect from the fact that it is a faculty of mind designed to deal with material objects, and one is able in that way to show the relation between intuition and intellect.

The importance of *Creative Evolution* is of this kind : It does not add anything new to Bergson's thought. If one has understood the difference between intensive and extensive manifolds, you have grasped the whole of that. That was all present in an embryo form, at any rate, in the first book. You could thoroughly understand the actually original part of Bergson without ever having read *Creative Evolution*. But what it actually does do—and this is, of course, no small achievement—is to plant all his ideas solidly down on the earth and show them at work before you in a concrete form, in physical shape. If one were to a certain extent rather exhausted by abstractions, this brings a certain relief. More than that, it gives a certain stability and ballast to the system.

CINDERS

A NEW WELTANSCHAUUNG

CINDERS

A Sketch of a New Weltanschauung

I. IN spite of pretensions to absolute truth, the results of philosophy are always tested by the effects, and by the judgments of other philosophers. There is always an appeal to a circle of people. The same is true of values in art, in morals. A man cannot stand alone on absolute ground, but always appeals to his fellows.

II. Therefore it is suggested that there is no such thing as an absolute truth to be discovered. All general statements about truth, etc., are in the end only amplifications of man's appetites.

The ultimate reality is a circle of persons, *i.e.* animals who communicate.

There is a kind of gossamer web, woven between the real things, and by this means the animals communicate. For purposes of communication they invent a symbolic language. Afterwards this language, used to excess, becomes a disease, and we get the curious phenomena of men explaining themselves by means of the gossamer web that connects them. Language becomes a disease in the hands of the counter-word mongers. It must constantly be remembered that it is an invention for the convenience of men ; and in the midst of Hegelians who triumphantly explain the world as a mixture of " good " and " beauty " and " truth," this should be remembered. What would an intelligent animal (without the language disease), or a carter in the road, think of it all ?

Symbols are picked out and believed to be realities. People imagine that all the complicated structure of the world can be woven out of " good " and " beauty." These words are merely counters representing vague groups of things, to be moved about on a board for the convenience of the players.

III. Objection might be taken that this makes man the measure of the world, and that after all he is only an animal, who came late, and the world must be supposed to have existed before he evolved at all. The reply to this is as follows :

(i) Analogy of courage and capacity. Courage in the Wild West requires capacities different from those it requires in the city. But the phenomena are the same : A non-muscular man is inevitably physically a coward.

(ii) The mental qualities of men and animals are common, though they are realised by different means.

(iii) These qualities—*e.g.* the common return to egoism, the roundness of the world, the absence of all infinitude, the denial of all Utopias—are extended to the ultimate nature of the world.

(iv) These qualities extend to the amœba and the inorganic world.

(v) It is these qualities with which the world is measured in § I.

(vi) Hence in a sense " Man is the measure of all things " and Man (egoism) *has always existed and always will exist.*

IV. Just as no common purpose can be aimed at for the conflicting purposes of real people, *so* there is no common purpose in the world.

The world is a plurality.

A unity arrived at by stripping off essentials is not a unity. Compound is not an inner reality.

V. This plurality consists in the nature of an ash-heap. In this ash-pit of cinders, certain ordered routes have been made, thus constituting whatever unity there may be—a kind of manufactured chess-board laid on a cinder-heap. Not a real chess-board impressed on the cinders, but the gossamer world of symbolic communication already spoken of.

CINDERS

THERE is a difficulty in finding a comprehensive scheme of the cosmos, because there is none. The cosmos is only *organised* in parts ; the rest is cinders.

Death is a breaking up into cinders. Hence partial truth of the old Greek conception of Hades (a place of less organisation and *no* happiness).

Many necessary conditions must be fulfilled before the counters and the chess-board can be posed elegantly on the cinders. Illness and death easily disturb and give falls from this condition. Perhaps this is an illustration of Nietzsche's image of the tight-rope walker. When all is arranged the counters are moved about. This is happiness, moving to enthusiastic conclusions, the musical note, perhaps Art. But it must be largely artificial. (Art prolongs it, and creates it by blur.)

The floating heroic world (built up of moments) and the cindery reality—can they be made to correspond to some fundamental constitution of the world ? (An antithesis much more deep than the one which analyses all realities into forms of egoism. This latter only a particular case of the general law.)

The *absolute* is to be described not as perfect, but if existent as essentially imperfect, chaotic, and cinder-like. (Even this view is not ultimate, but merely designed to satisfy temporary human analogies and wants.)

World is indescribable, that is, not reducible to counters ; and particularly it is impossible to include it all under one large counter such as " God " or " Truth " and the other verbalisms, or the disease of the symbolic language.

Cinders can never be counters except for certain practical purposes (good enough)— cf. rail lines and chess-board. The treatment of the soul as the central part of the nominalist position. Their habit of regarding it as a kind of round counter all red, which survives *whole* in all its redness and roundness (the redness as the character), a counter-like *distinct* separate entity, just as *word* itself is.

Why is it that London looks pretty by night ? Because for the general cindery chaos there is substituted a simple ordered arrangement of a finite number of lights.

The two complementary phenomena : that each wash is a line, and that each line is a wash.

That the world is finite (atomism : there are no infinitudes except in art) and that it is yet an infinitude of cinders (there is no finite law encompassing all).

This new view may perhaps be caricatured by saying that the bad is fundamental, and that the good is artificially built up in it and out of it, like oases in the desert, or as cheerful houses in the storm.

(Two parts : 1—All cinders ; 2—the part built up. So the question : How far built up and how far given us ? The question of the pliability of the world.)

All is flux. The moralists, the capital letterists, attempt to find a framework outside the flux, a solid bank for the river, a pier rather than a raft. Truth is what helps a particular sect in the general flow.

School children at a fountain (moved mechanically by thirst) to someone looking down from above, appear as a pure instinctive mechanical act. Cf. ants—we are unable to ascertain the subtler reasons which move them. They all look alike. Hence humpty-dumpty's remark about human faces is seen to be the foundation of all science and all philosophy.

Only in the fact of consciousness is there a unity in the world. Cf. Oxford Street at 2 A.M.

All the mud, endless, except where bound together by the spectator.

Unity is made in the world by drawing squares over it. We are able to get along these at any rate—cf. railway line in desert. (Always the elusive as seen in maps. *Ad infinitum.*)

The squares include cinders—always cinders.

No unity of laws, but merely of the sorting machine.

Formerly, one liked theories because they reduced the world to a single principle. Now the same reason disgusts us. The flats of Canada are incomprehensible on any single theory. The world only comprehensible on the cinder theory.

The same old fallacy persists—the desire to introduce a unity in the world : (1) The mythologists made it a woman or an elephant : (2) The scientists made fun of the mythologists, but themselves turned the world into the likeness of a mechanical toy. They were more concerned with models than with woman (woman troubled them and hence their particular form of anthropomorphism). One analogy is as good as another. The truth remains that the world is not any unity, but a house in the cinders (outside in the cold, primeval).

Contrast the Pythagorean ecstasies in the numbers 3 and 7. The cinder is the opposite prejudice. I am immediately up in arms if a book says a subject can be divided into three separate parts.

Most of our life is spent in buttoning and unbuttoning. Yes, quite so. This fact can be welcomed as fitting in with the general theory.

The unity of Nature is an extremely artificial and fragile bridge, a garden net.

The covers of a book are responsible for much error. They set a limit round certain convenient groups of ideas, when there are really no limits.

The aim of science and of all thought is to reduce the complex and inevitably disconnected world of grit and cinders to a few ideal counters, which we can move about and so form an ungritlike picture of reality—one flattering to our sense of power over the world.

In the end this is true too of mathematics, though at first it appears as a more complex symbolism. The conclusion of all mathematics is : That one counter stands in a certain relation to another. That counter may be a simple number or an elliptic integral, but the final effect is the same. (All mathematics is deducible from numbers, which are nothing but counters.)

CINDERS

There is an *objective* world (?), a chaos, a cinder-heap. Gradually oases have been built up. Egos have grown as organised trees.

So not *idealist*, as that assumes that there is nothing but a fixed number of persons, and without them nothing. (So the Real New Realism is something beyond names. World can't be O because O is opposed to human psychology.)

A landscape, with occasional oases. So now and then we are moved—at the theatre, action, a love. But mainly deserts of dirt, ash-pits of the cosmos, grass on ash-pits. No universal ego, but a few definite persons gradually built up.

Nature as the accumulation of the memories of man.

Certain groups of ideas as huts for men to live in. The Act of Creation.

Truth is always seen to lie in a compromise. All clear cut ideas turn out to be wrong. Analogy to real things, which are artificially picked out of the general lava flow of cinders.

Cf. the wandering attention in the library. Sometimes one seems to have definite clear cut moments, but not afterwards.

I. Nature. Scenery as built up by man. Oases in the desert of grit.

II. Extended to the whole of the world.

III. *But* the microscope. Things revealed, not created, but there before, and *also* seem to be in an order.

IV. Before man other powers created in the struggle.

V. So man was gradually built up, and man's world was gradually built up at the same time.

Evolution of colour; dim perception of it in the amœba; evolved—the whole modern world of colour built up from this; gradually made more counter-like and distinct.

There is no inevitable order into which ideas must be shifted.

We live in a room, of course, but the great question for philosophy is: how far have we decorated the room, and how far was it made before we came? Did we merely decorate the room, or did we make it from chaos? The laws of nature that we certainly do find —what are they?

In an organised city it is not easy to see the cinder element of earth—all is banished. But it is easy to see it psychologically. What the Nominalists call the grit in the machine, I call the fundamental element of the machine.

Properly to estimate the true purpose of absolute philosophy, it should be realised as reducing everything to number, the only rational and logical solution from the point of view that dares to conceive relation as of more importance than the persons related.

The eyes, the beauty of the world, have been organised out of the fæces. Man returns to dust. So does the face of the world to primeval cinders.

A girl's ball-dress and shoes are symbolic of the world organised (in counters) from the mud. Separate from contact.

Only the isolated points seem to have any value, so how can the world be said to be designed ? Rather we may say that gradually certain points are being designed.

Taken *mystically*—then all peculiarities of the human organism must have their counterpart in the construction of the world.

E.g.—Illness and a reversion to chaos.

Man is the chaos highly organised, but liable to revert to chaos at any moment. Happiness and ecstasy at present unstable. Walking in the street, seeing pretty girls (all chaos put into the drains : not seen) and wondering what they would look like ill. Men laughing at a bar—but wait till the fundamental chaos reveals itself.

The two moods in life. (i) Ill in bed, toothache, W.C. in the Atlantic—the disor-

ganised, withdrawn-into-oneself mood. (ii)
Flying along in the wind (wind in the hair, on
a motor bus). *Or* evolving a new theory.
The impersonal feeling.

Ennui and disgust, the sick moments—not
an occasional lapse or disease, but the fundamental ennui and chaos out of which the
world has been built, and which is as necessary
to it as the listeners are to intellectuals. The
old world order of queens and pawns.

The apparent scientific unity of the world
may be due to the fact that man is a kind of
sorting machine.

" I must tell someone " as the final criterion
of philosophy, the *raison d'être* of the human
circle symbol.

The sick disgusting moments are part of the
fundamental cinders — primeval chaos — the
dream of impossible chaos.

The absolute is invented to reconcile conflicting purposes. But these purposes are
necessarily conflicting, even in the nature of
Truth itself. It is so absurd to construct an
absolute which shall at each moment just
manage by artificial gymnastics to reconcile
these purposes.

Philosophical syntheses and ethical systems
are only possible in arm-chair moments. They

are seen to be meaningless as soon as we get into a bus with a dirty baby and a crowd.

Note the fact that all a writer's generalisations and truths can be traced to the personal circumstances and prejudices of his class, experience, capacity and body. This, however, is not an instance of error or hypocrisy. There is no average or real truth to be discerned among the different fronts of prejudice. Each is a truth in so far as it satisfies the writer.

We must judge the world from the status of animals, leaving out " Truth," etc.

Animals are in the same state that men were before symbolic language was invented.

Philosophy is about people in clothes, not about the soul of man.

The fixed order of the world is woven in a gigantic way by the acts of men and animals.

The world lives in order to develop the lines on its face.

These little theories of the world, which satisfy and are then thrown away, one after the other, develop *not* as successive approximations to the truth, but like successive thirsts, to be satisfied at the moment, and not evolving to one great Universal Thirst.

Through all the ages, the conversation of ten men sitting together is what holds the world together.

Never think in a book : here are Truth and all the other capital letters ; but think in a theatre and watch the audience. Here is the reality, here are human animals. Listen to the words of heroism and then at the crowded husbands who applaud. All philosophies are subordinate to this. It is not a question of the unity of the world and men afterwards put into it, *but* of human animals, and of philosophies as an elaboration of their appetites.

Words.

Heaven as the short summary paradise of words.

The ideal of knowledge : all cinders reduced to counters (words) ; these counters moved about on a chess-board, and so all phenomena made obvious.

Something is always lost in generalisation. A railway leaves out all the gaps of dirt between. Generalisations are only means of getting about.

Cf. the words love, sex, nude, with the actual details.

I hate more than anything the vague long pretentious words of Wells—" indefinable tendency in events," etc., etc.

Always seek the hard, definite, personal word.

The real levelheadedness : to be able to analyse a pretty girl at first sight, not to be intoxicated with clothes, to be able to imagine the effect of dipping in water—this is what one must be able to do for words, and for all embracing philosophies. We must not be taken in by the arm-chair moments.

The World is Round.

Disillusionment comes when it is recognised that all heroic actions can be reduced to the simple laws of egoism. But wonder can even then be found in the fact that there *are* such *different* and *clear-cut* laws and egoisms and that they have been created out of the chaos.

The pathetic search for the *different*. Where shall they find it ? Never found in sex. All explored sex is the same.

World as finite, and so no longer any refuge in infinities of grandeur.

Atomism.

Resolution of apparent flexibility and continuity into atomic structure. Oratory and fluency mean a collection of phrases at fingers' ends. This seen in Hyde Park, the young men, Christian preachers.

SPECULATIONS

Escapes to the infinite :

   (i) Art.   Blur, strangeness, music.

   (ii) Sentimentality.

The sentimental illusion of a man (invalid) who takes pleasure in resting his head in a woman's lap—it is a deliberate act, work on her part. While he may feel the sentimental escape to the infinite, she has to be uncomfortable and prosaic.

All experience tends to do away with all sentimental escapes to the infinite, but at the same time to provide many deliberated, observed, manufactured, artificial, spectacular, poised for seeing continuities and patterns.

The universal conspiracy : other people unconsciously provide the sentimental spectacle in which you luxuriate. The world *is* nothing more or less than a stage.

There may be an attitude which sees that most things are illusions, that experience is merely the gradual process of disillusionment, that the new as well as the old ideals turn out to be partial, non-continuous or infinite, but then in face of this decides that certain illusions or moods are pleasurable and exhilarating, and deliberately and knowingly encourages them. A judicious choice of illusions, leading to activities planned and carried out, is the only means of happiness, *e.g.* the exhilaration of regarding life as a procession or a war.

CINDERS

In opposition to socialism and utopian schemes comes the insistence on the fact of the unalterability of motives. Motives are the only unalterable and fixed things in the world. They extend to the animal kingdom. They are the only *rock*: physical bases change. They are more than *human* motives: they are the constitution of the world.

That great secret which all men find out for themselves, and none reveal—or if they do, like Cassandra, are not believed—that the world is round. The young man refuses to believe it.

Refuse World as a unit and take Person (in flight from the word fallacy).

But why person? Why is the line drawn exactly there in the discussion of counter words?

We are becoming so particular in the choice of words and the rejection of symbolisms that we are in danger of *forgetting* that the world does really exist.

The truth is that there are no ultimate principles, upon which the whole of knowledge can be built once and for ever as upon a rock. But there are an infinity of analogues, which help us along, and give us a feeling of power over the chaos when we perceive them. The field is infinite and herein lies the chance for originality. Here there are some new things under the sun. (Perhaps it would be better to say that there are some new things under the moon, for here is the land pre-eminently of shadows, fancies and analogies.)

Danger.

One must recognise thought's essential independence of the imagery that steadies it. Subtle associations which familiar images recall are insinuated into the thought.

Though perhaps we do not realise it, we are still governed by the analogy, by which spirit was first compared to the wind. The contrast the same as the one between the little box and space, between the court and cinders —that between the one that thinks of a man as an elaborately built up pyramid, a constructed elaboration, easily upset and not flexible, only functioning in one direction, the one in which he was made, and the other that considers him as a flexible essence, a spirit, like a *fluid*.

We can all see that there is an eternal flexibility in the most obviously constituted man, but we realise the contrast best when looking at a tailor's model of a man in dress, whose limbs move and flex.

In the problem of ghosts which bend and flex lies the whole difference between the two world philosophies—

CINDERS

I. Flexible essence.

II. Built up stuff.

Philosophical Jargon.

There is this consoling thought, supporting us while wandering in the wilderness of which the priests alone pretend they have the secret. In all other uses of language, no matter for what purpose, the analogies used are quite simple, and even can be replaced, leaving the idea behind them just as real. The analogies a man uses to represent a state of soul, though personal, can be replaced, to produce almost the same effect. *No one* mistakes the analogies for the real thing they stand for.

The Dancer.

Dancing to express the organisation of cinders, finally emancipated (cf. bird).

I sat before a stage and saw a little girl with her head thrown back, and a smile. I knew her, for she was the daughter of John of Elton.

But she smiled, and her feet were not like feet, but . . . . . [sic].

Though I knew her body.

All these sudden insights (*e.g.* the great analogy of a woman compared to the world in Brussels)—all of these start a line, which seems about to unite the whole world logically. But the line stops. There is no unity. All logic and life are made up of tangled ends like that.

Always think of the fringe and of the cold walks, of the lines that lead nowhere.

Mind and Matter.

Realise that to take *one* or the *other* as absolute is to perpetrate the same old counter fallacy ; both are mixed up in a cindery way and we extract them as counters.

Mathematics takes one group of counters, abstracts them and makes them absolute, down to Matter and Motion.

That *fringe of cinders* which bounds any ecstasy.

The tall lanky fellow, with a rose, in a white moonlit field. But where does he sleep ?

All heroes, great men, go to the outside, away from the Room, and wrestle with cinders.

And cinders become the Azores, the Magic Isles.

A house built is then a symbol, a Roman Viaduct ; but the walk there and the dirt— this must jump right into the mind also.

Aphra's Finger.

There are moments when the tip of one's finger seems raw. In the contact of it and the world there seems a strange difference. The spirit lives on that tip and is thrown on the rough cinders of the world. All philosophy depends on that—the state of the tip of the finger.

When Aphra had touched, even lightly, the rough wood, this wood seemed to cling to his finger, to draw itself backward and forward along it. The spirit returned again and again, as though fascinated, to the luxurious torture of the finger.

The prediction of the stars is no more wonderful, and no more accurate than the prediction of another person's conduct. There is no last refuge here for the logical structure of the world.

The phenomenon we study is not the immense world in our hand, but certain little observations we make about it. We put these on a table and look at them.

We study little chalk marks on a table (chalk because that shows the cindery nature of the division we make) and create rules near enough for them.

If we look at a collection of cinders from all directions, in the end, we are bound to find a shadow that looks regular.

The attempt to get a common element in personality, *i.e.* the old attempt to get a unity. Abstract an element and call that a fundamental.

The inner spirit of the world is miles and miles of ploughed fields.

Never speak of " my unconquerable soul," or of any vulgarism of that sort. But thank God for the long note of the bugle, which moves all the world bodily out of the cinders and the mud.

There is only one *art* that moves me : architecture.

French.

The exact fault which is typical of French books : The taking of a few opinions, a few epigrams, a few literary *obiter dicta*, and arranging them symmetrically, finding a logical order, an underlying principle where there is one, and calling the whole a science.

I shall call my philosophy the " Valet to the Absolute." The Absolute not a hero to his own valet.

All these various little notes will never combine because in their nature they cannot. The facts of Nature are solid enough, but Man is a weathercock standing in the middle, looking first at one part and then at another. A little idea in one sentence appears to contain a whole new world philosophy. So it does. But then a world philosophy is only a certain direction, N. or S. It is quite easy to change this direction. Hence the astonishing power that philosophers appear to have at the summit of the sciences. Buy a book obviously literary, by an amateur, made of light combinations of words. It seems to change the world, but nothing is further from the truth. It just turns the weathercock to a new direction. The philosophic faculty is quite irresponsible, the easiest moving thing in nature, and quite divorced from nature.

So be sceptical of the first enthusiasm that a new idea gives.

The Eagle's eye.

The ruling analogy, which is quite false, must be removed. It is that of the eagle's eye. The metaphysician imagines that he surveys the world as with an eagle's eye. And the farther he flies, the " purer " his knowledge becomes.

Hence we can see the world as pure geometry, and can make out its dividing lines.

But the eye is in the mud, the eye *is* mud.

Pure seeing of the whole process is impossible. Little fancies help us along, but we never get pure disinterested intellect.

Space.

I. Admitted the pragmatic criterion of any analogy that makes for clearness.

II. Now *space* is essential to clearness. A developed notion, perhaps, but now essential.

III. The idealists analyse space into a mode of arranging sensations. But this gives us an unimaginable world existing all at a point.

IV. Why not try the reverse process and put all ideas (purely mental states) into terms of *space* (cf. landscape thinking) ?

The sense of reality is inevitably connected with that of *space* (the world existing before us).

Truths don't exist before we invent them. They respond to man's need of economy, just as beliefs to his need of faith.

The fountain turned on. It has a definite geometrical shape, but the shape did not exist before it was turned on. Compare the arguments about the pre-existence of the soul.

But the little pipes are there before, which give it that shape as soon as the water is turned on.

The water is the same though the geometrical figures of different fountains differ.

By analogy we may perhaps claim that there is no such thing as a personal soul. The personality of the soul depends on the bodily frame which receives it, *i.e.* on the shape of the pipes.

The soul is a spirit certainly, but undifferentiated and without personality. The personality is given by the bodily frame which receives and shapes it.

Ritual and sentiment.

Sentiment cannot easily retire into itself in pure thought; it cannot live and feed on itself for very long. In wandering, thought is easily displaced by other matters. So that the man who deliberately sets himself the task of thinking continuously of a lover or dead friend has an impossible task. He is inevitably drawn to some form of ritual for the expression and outflow of the sentiment. Some act which requires less concentration, and which at an easy level fulfils his obligations to sentiment, which changes a morbid feeling into a grateful task and employment. Such as pilgrimages to graves, standing bareheaded and similar freaks of a lover's fancy. The same phenomena can be observed in religion. A man cannot deliberately make up his mind to think of the goodness of God for an hour, but he can perform some ritual act of admiration whether it be the offering of a sacrifice or merely saying amen to a set prayer. Ritual tends to be constant, even that seeming exception the impromptu prayers of a Non-conformist minister are merely the stringing together in accidental order of set and well-known phrases and tags. The burning of candles to the Virgin if only one can escape from some danger. The giving of a dinner, or getting drunk in company as a celebration—a relief from concentrated thinking.

Body.

In Tube lift hearing the phrase " fed up,"
and realising that all our analogies spiritual
and intellectual are derived from purely
physical acts. Nay more, all attributes of the
absolute and the abstract are really nothing
more (in so far as they mean anything) but
elaborations of simple passions.

All poetry is an affair of the body—that is,
to be real it must affect body.

Action.

Teachers, university lecturers on science,
emancipated women, and other spectacled
anæmics attending the plays at the Court
Theatre remind me of disembodied spirits,
having no body to rest in. They have all the
intellect and imagination required for high
passion, but no material to work on. They
feel all the emotions of jealousy and desire,
but these leading to no action remain as
nothing but petty motives. *Passion is action*
and without action but a child's anger.

They lack the bodies and the daggers.
Tragedy never sits steadily on a chair, except
in certain vague romantic pictures which are
thus much affected (as real tragedy) by the
moderns and the sedentary. Just as sentiment and religion require expression in ritual,
so tragedy requires action.

Jealousy, desire to kill, desire for strong

arms and knives, resolution to shake off social convention and to do it.

The knife order.

Why grumble because there is no end discoverable in the world? There is no end at all except in our own constructions.

Necessity of distinguishing between a vague philosophic statement that " reality always escapes a system," and the definite cinder, felt in a religious way and being a criterion of nearly all judgment, philosophic and æsthetic.

No Geist without ghost.

This the only truth in the subject.

Is there here a possible violation of the cinder principle; an escape back to the old fallacy? But without some definite assertion of this kind. . . . Some definite crossing beyond is necessary to escape poetic overstatement, to relieve us.

Philosophy.

The strange quality, shade of feeling, one gets (a few people alone in a position a little separated from the world); a ship's cabin, the last bus.

If all the world were destroyed and only these left. . . . That all the gods, all the winged words (love . . .) exist *in them* on that fluid basis.

To take frankly that fluid basis and elaborate it into a solidity, that the gods do not exist horizontally in space but somehow vertically in the isolated fragment of the tribe. There is another form of space where gods, etc., do exist concretely.

Smoothness.

Hate it.
This is the obsession that starts all my theories.
Get other examples, other facets of the one idea.
Build them up by catalogue method

(I) in science ;

(II) in sex ;

(III) in poetry.

Analogy.

I look at the reality, at London stream, and dirt, mud, power, and then I think of the pale shadowy analogy that is used without thinking by the automatic philosophers, the " stream of time." The people who treat words without reverence, who use analogies without thinking of them : let us always remember that solid real stream and the flat thin voice of the metaphysician, " *the stream of time.*"

Extended clay. Looking at the Persian

Gulf on a map and imagining the mud shore at night.

Pictures of low coasts of any country. We are all just above the sea.

Delight in perceiving the real cinder construction in a port. Upon mud as distinct from the clear-cut harbour on the map.

Travel is education in cinders; the merchants in Hakluyt, and the difference in song. (When we are all gathered together and when we are in a book.)

Must see these different manifestations of the cinders; otherwise we cannot work the extended clay.

A melancholy spirit, the mind like a great desert lifeless, and the sound of march music in the street, passes like a wave over that desert, unifies it, but then goes.

APPENDICES

APPENDIX A

REFLECTIONS ON VIOLENCE

. . . que si par impossible, la nature avait fait de l'homme un animal exclusivement industrieux et sociable, et point guerrier, il serait tombé, dès le premier jour, au niveau des bêtes dont l'association forme toute la destinée ; il aurait perdu, avec l'orgueil de son héroisme, sa faculté révolutionnaire, la plus merveilleuse de toutes, et la plus féconde. Vivant en communauté pure, notre civilisation serait une étable. . . . Philanthrope, vous parlez d'abolir la guerre, prenez garde de dégrader le genre humain. . . . *Proudhon.*

NEARLY all the criticism of Sorel's work goes wrong, not so much in details as in its complete inability to understand its main motive ; the sympathetic accounts being as irritating and as wide of the mark as the others.

What exactly is the nature of this general miscomprehension ? In a movement like socialism we can conveniently separate out two distinct elements, the working-class movement itself and the system of ideas which goes with it (though the word is ugly, it will be convenient to follow Sorel and call a system of ideas an *ideology*). If we call one (I) and the other (W), (I + W) will be the whole movement. The ideology is, as a matter of fact,

249

*democracy.** Now the enormous difficulty in
Sorel comes in this—that he not only denies
the essential connection between these two
elements, but even asserts that the ideology
will be fatal to the movement. The regeneration of society will never be brought by the
pacifist *progressives*.

They may be pardoned then if they find
this strange. This combination of doctrines
which they would probably call reactionary,
with revolutionary syndicalism, is certainly
very disconcerting to liberal Socialists. It is
difficult for them to understand a revolutionary who is anti-democratic, an absolutist
in ethics, rejecting all rationalism and relativism, who values the mystical element in
religion " which will never disappear," speaks
contemptuously of modernism and *progress*,
and uses a concept like *honour* with no sense
of unreality.†

As a rule such sentiments, when the *demo-*

* *Democracy*—the word is not used here either (1) as a general
name for the working-class movement or (2) to indicate the true
doctrine that all men are equal. It is not used then in its widest
sense as indicating opposition to all aristocratic, oligarchic or
class government, but in a narrower sense, to recall which I have
always put the word in italics. Liberal might have been a better
word, were it not that Socialists, while proclaiming their difference
from liberalism in policy, at the same time adopt the whole
liberal *ideology ;* and though they do not acknowledge it to be
liberal, they will recognise it under the label *democratic*.

† An *ideology* naturally includes a system of sentiments. In
this respect the book is even more confusing to the democrat than
in that of ideas. The divergence in sentiments is most striking,
however, in what Sorel says about the feelings of envy and retalia-
tion as the basis of liberal *democracy*. A careful analysis of this
sentiment and its historical connection with democracy can be
found in Max Scheler's *Über Ressentiment u. Werttheorie*.

crat meets with them, are conveniently dismissed as springing from a disguised attempt to defend the interests of wealth. But this obviously will not fit the case of Sorel. There is then some danger of a foreign body lodging itself inside the system of democratic thought. The latter deals with this irritant, very much as one would expect. It calls to its aid the righteous indignation which every *real progressive* must feel at the slightest suspicion of anything *reactionary*. Instead of considering the details of the actual thesis, the *progressive* prefers to discredit it by an imagined origin. Sorel's attitude is thus attributed to mysticism, to neo-royalism, or to some confused and sentimental reaction against Reason. This summary dismissal is accompanied by a distinct feeling of relief. " You see there is nothing in it. It is only our old adversaries in a new disguise." The people who make this kind of criticism are clearly incapable of understanding the main thesis of the book. The misunderstanding will be very stubborn. How can it be removed ?

The first step is to note more exactly the feelings of the simple-minded democrat towards this thesis. His behaviour may indicate the source of his repugnance, and give some hints as to its removal. What he mostly feels, I suppose, is a kind of exasperation. He cannot take the *anti-democratic* view seriously. He feels just as if some one had denied one of the laws of thought, or asserted that two and two are five. In his natural state, of course, he never thinks of the movement as composed of two elements (I + W). It is one undivided whole for him. When, however, the denial of the connection between I and W forces the separate existence of (I) on his notice, he at once thinks of it, not as one possible *ideology* amongst others, but as an *inevitable* way of thinking, which must necessarily accompany (W) as it accompanies everything.

It is this notion of the *necessary*, the inevitable character of the *democratic* system of ideas, which is here the stumbling-block. It is this which makes him think Sorel's *anti-democratic* position and views *unnatural* or perverse. He has not yet thought of *democracy* as a system at all, but only as a natural and inevitable equipment of the emancipated and instructed man. The ideas which underlie it appear to him to have the *necessary* character of categories. In reality they are, of course, nothing of the kind. They depend on certain fundamental attitudes of the mind, on unexpressed major premises. If he could be made conscious of these premises, the character of inevitability would have been removed. The explanation of how these major premises get into the position of *pseudo-categories* goes a long way towards removing a man from their influence. They are unperceived because they have become so much part of the mind and lie so far back that we are never really conscious of them as ideas at all. We do not see them, but see other things *through* them, and consequently take what we see for the outlines of things themselves. Blue spectacles making a blue world can be pointed out, but not these pseudo-categories which lie, as it were, " behind the eye."

All effective propaganda depends then on getting these ideas away from their position " behind the eye " and putting them facing one as *objects* which we can then consciously accept or reject. This is extremely difficult. Fortunately, however, all ideologies are of gradual growth, and that rare type of historical intelligence which investigates and analyses their origins can help us considerably. Just as a knowledge of the colours extended and separated in the spectrum enables us to analyse the feebler colours confused together in shadows, so this type of history, by exhibiting certain ideas in a concreter form, existing as it were as objects in time, enables us to distinguish the same ideas, existing in us " behind the eye " and to bring them to the surface of the mind. Their hidden influence on our opinions then at once disappears, for they have lost their status as categories. This is a violent operation, and the mind is never quite the same afterwards. It has lost a certain virginity. But there are so many of these systems in which we unwittingly " live and move and have our being " that the process really forms the major part of the education of the adult. Moreover the historical method by exhibiting the intimate connection between such conceptions—that of *Progress* for example—and certain economical conditions at the time of their invention in the eighteenth century, does more than anything else to loosen their hold over the mind. It is this method which Sorel has so successfully applied in *Les Illusions du Progrés* to the particular democratic ideology, with which we are here concerned.

This *democratic* ideology * is about two centuries old. Its history can be clearly followed, and its logical connection with a parallel movement in literature. It is an essential element in the romantic movement ; it forms an organic body of middle-class thought dating from the eighteenth century, and has consequently no necessary connection whatever with the working-class or revolutionary movement. Liberal Socialism is still living on the remains of middle-class thought of the last century. When vulgar thought of to-day is pacifist, rationalist, and hedonist, and in being so believes itself to be expressing

---

* The opposed ideology in Sorel can most conveniently be described by thinking of the qualities of seventeenth as contrasted with eighteenth century literature in France, the difference, for example, between Corneille and Diderot. Sorel often speaks of Cornelian virtue. But the antithesis of Classical and Romantic is not enough to make the *Classical* comprehensible to a *Romantic ;* it is necessary to get down to the two fundamental attitudes from which the difference really springs.

the inevitable convictions of the instructed and emancipated man, it has all the pathos of marionettes in a play, dead things gesticulating as though they were alive. Our younger novelists, like those Roman fountains in which water pours from the mouth of a human mask, gush as though spontaneously from the depths of their own being, a muddy romanticism that has in reality come through a very long pipe.

Democratic romanticism is then a body of doctrine with a recognisable and determinate history. What is the central attitude from which it springs, and which gives it continued life ? What is the unexpressed major premise here ?

Putting the matter with the artificial simplicity of a diagram for the sake of clearness, we might say that romanticism and classical pessimism differ in their antithetical conception of the nature of man. For the one, man is by nature good, and for the other, by nature bad.

All Romanticism springs from Rousseau,* and the key to it can be found even in the first sentence of the Social Contract—"Man is born free, and he finds himself everywhere in chains." In other words, man is by nature something wonderful, of unlimited powers, and if hitherto he has not appeared so, it is

* For a history of the romantic movement in French Literature from this point of view, see Pierre Lasserre's excellent *La Romantisme française.*

because of external obstacles and fetters, which it should be the main business of social politics to remove.

What is at the root of the contrasted system of ideas you find in Sorel, the classical, pessimistic, or, as its opponents would have it, the reactionary ideology ? This system springs from the exactly contrary conception of man ; the conviction that man is by nature bad or limited,* and can consequently only accomplish anything of value by disciplines, ethical, heroic, or political. In other words, it believes in Original Sin. We may define Romantics, then, as all who do not believe in the Fall of Man. It is this opposition which in reality lies at the root of most of the other divisions in social and political thought.†

* This is by no means identical with materialism ; rather it is characteristic of the religious attitude—cf. Pascal's *Pensées*. Romanticism confuses both human and divine things by not clearly separating them. The main thing with which it can be reproached is that it blurs the clear outlines of human relations—whether in political thought or in the treatment of sex in literature, by introducing into them the Perfection that properly belongs only to the non-human.

† Not only here but in philosophy itself ; this can be made clear by a parallel. The change of sensibility which has enabled us to appreciate Egyptian, Indian, Byzantine, Polynesian, and Negro work as *art* and not as archæology or ethnology, has a double effect. While it demonstrates that what were taken for the necessary principles of æsthetics are merely a psychology of Classical and modern European art, it at the same time suddenly forces us to see the essential unity of this art. In spite of its apparent variety, European art in reality forms a coherent body of work resting on certain presuppositions, of which we become conscious for the first time when we see them denied by other periods of art (cf. the work of Riegl on Byzantine art). One might say that in the same way, an understanding of the religious philosophy which subordinates man (regarded as a part of nature) to certain absolute values—in other words, a realisation of the

REFLECTIONS ON VIOLENCE

From the pessimistic conception of man comes naturally the view that the transformation of society is an heroic task requiring heroic qualities . . . virtues which are not likely to flourish on the soil of a rational and sceptical ethic. This regeneration can, on the contrary, only be brought about and only be maintained by actions springing from an ethic which from the narrow rationalist standpoint is irrational, being not *relative*, but absolute.*
The transformation of society is not likely to

sense of this dogma—forces us to see that there is a much greater family resemblance between all philosophy since the Renaissance than is ever recognised. The philosophy rests, in reality, on the same presuppositions as the art, and forms a coherent system with it. It seems as if no sooner had Copernicus shown that man was not the centre of the universe, than the philosophers commenced for the first time to prove that he was. You get expressed explicitly, for the first time (in Pico della Mirandola for example), this idea of the sufficiency of natural man, and it has generally been assumed by all philosophers since. It may be expressed in very different languages and with very different degrees of profundity, but even Hegel and Condorcet are one, from this point of view. Humanism thus really contains the germs of the disease that was bound to come to its full evil development in Romanticism.

It is promising to note signs of the break-up of this period in art, and there are some slight indications of a corresponding anti-humanistic movement in thought and ethics. (G. E. Moore, Duguit, Husserl and " Phaenomenologie.")

* *Virtue.*—Without too much exaggeration it might be said that the objective and absolute view of ethics to which Sorel adheres has at the present moment more chance of being understood. There has always been something rather unreal about ethics. In a library one's hand glided over books on that subject instinctively. That is, perhaps, because the only ethical questions that came before parasitical literary men were those of sex, in which (may I be forgiven, being here no disciple of Sorel) there seems very little but expediency, nothing that a man could honestly feel objective. But many sensualists lately have had to make an ethical decision for the first time, and uncomfortably recognise that as there is one objective thing at least in ethics, so there may be many more.

be achieved as a result of peaceful and intelligent *readjustment* on the part of literary men and politicians. But on the optimistic and romantic view this is quite possible. For the optimistic conception of man leads naturally to the characteristic democratic doctrine of inevitable *Progress*.

An understanding of the classical side of this antithesis entirely removes the strangeness of Sorel's position. But though this tendency can be seen, even in his earlier work (the first book on Socrates maintaining that Socrates represents the decadence in Athens, having introduced expediency and calculation into ethics)—yet his final disillusionment with *democracy* came only after the bitter experience of political events which followed the Dreyfus case. A good part of the book consequently is concerned with people who are to us somewhat obscure. But it should be remembered that these obscure figures all have their counterparts here, and that the drama they figure in is a universal one.

The belief that pacifist democracy will lead to no regeneration of society, but rather to its decadence, and the reaction against romanticism in literature, is naturally common to many different schools. This is the secret, for example, of the sympathy between Sorel and the group of writers connected with *L'Action française*, which is so eagerly fastened on by those anxious to discredit him. His *ideology* resembles theirs. Where he differs is in the application he finds for it. He expects a return of the classical spirit through the struggle of the classes.* This is the part of his thesis that is concerned with facts, and it would be impertinent on my part to offer any commentary on it. I have been only concerned with certain misapprehensions about the purely theoretical part of his thesis.† One may note here, however, how he makes the two interact. Given the classical attitude, he tries to prove that its present manifestation may be hoped for in working-class violence, and at the same time the complementary notion that only under the influence of the classical ideal will the movement succeed in regenerating society.

Sorel is one of the most remarkable writers of the time, certainly the most remarkable socialist since Marx; and his influence is likely to increase, for, in spite of the apparently undisturbed supremacy of rationalist hedonism in popular thought, the *absolute* view of ethics which underlies his polemic, is

---

* It is this which differentiates Sorel's from other attacks on the democratic *ideology*. Some of these are merely dilettante, having little sense of reality, while others are really vicious, in that they play with the idea of inequality. No theory that is not fully moved by the conception of justice asserting the equality of men, and which cannot offer something to all men, deserves or is likely to have any future.

† In doing this I have laid a disproportionate emphasis on one aspect of Sorel. I have not endeavoured, however, to give any general account of his work here, but only to remove the most probable cause of misunderstanding. Otherwise, I should have liked to have noted his relations to Marx, Proudhon, and to Vico, and also to have said something of his conception of history, of which Croce has written in the preface to the Italian translation.

gradually being re-established. A similar combination of the classical ideal with socialism is to be found, it is true, in Proudhon, but Sorel comes at a happier moment. The *ideology* attacked by Proudhon has now reached a fuller development, and its real consequences can be more easily perceived. There are many who begin to be disillusioned with liberal and pacifist *democracy*, while shrinking from the opposed *ideology* on account of its reactionary associations. To these people Sorel, a revolutionary in economics, but classical in ethics, may prove an emancipator.

APPENDIX B

THE PLAN FOR A BOOK

on

Modern Theories of Art

1. BIBLIOGRAPHY : Italian, French, German, and English.

2. SHORT INTRODUCTION.

3. CHAPTER I.—Most attractive and most neglected part of philosophy—its unhappy fate : left either to (1) the technical philosophers who knowing nothing of art have made it fit into their systems —or to (2) the amateurs of all periods who knowing little of philosophy have used the inaccurate concepts and metaphors of a merely literary method.

SPECULATIONS

Critical anarchy—plea for the systematic study of the subject.

At the present moment this unhappy state at an end—sudden and remarkable development of the subject—rich harvest of theories in Germany—the characteristic feature of modern German philosophy—practical creation of a new subject—this astonishing and intensely interesting literature entirely unknown in England.

Causes of this—the development of modern psychology enables subject for first time to be treated in systematic instead of amateur way.

CHAPTER 2.—*Short historical sketch.* Plato, Aristotle, Baumgarten, English 18th-century writers, German idealist theories.

Kant, Schelling, Hegel ; influence on English romantics. Coleridge, Shelley, etc., Ruskin.

Modern beginning of the subject. Vischer, Fechner, Groos, Guyau, etc. The foundations of the schools treated in this book.

CHAPTER 3.—*Preliminary inquiry :* to show treatment of subject in this book. Complicated mixture of different questions involved in question " What is Art ? "—this mixed question must be analysed into several separate and distinct questions.

Method (*a*) Taking modern arts as known, ask this question—Is there any specific emotion which characterises them all and found in no other activity ?—a specifically æsthetic emotion, the experiencing of which constitutes beauty— the sceptical answer to this question—the affirmative—if there is, then what is the nature of this emotion, how can it be defined ; this the problem of æsthetics and the one this book principally deals with.

(*b*) The entirely different inquiry—the psychology of artistic creation—what is the nature of state of mind characterised as creative imagination—Ribot—this the subject of much merely literary inquiry—examples—now for first time rough analyses which artists themselves have given can be interpreted in the light of new psychology—Bergson.

(c) Most discussed question—Is art independent or subordinate to human activities and needs? —Kant, Nietzsche, Tolstoy, etc.—though really outside æsthetics proper, yet has bearing on question in (b), for if art is merely a means of conveying ordinary human emotion, then it cannot be defined by any specific æsthetic emotion —in this region come old disputes—romantic, classic, etc.

This book principally concerned with (a) and (b). Principal modern theories examined bearing in mind this analysis of the questions involved.

CHAPTER 4.—*French—Bergson :* statement of the theory and its origins—Séailles, Guyau, Ribot, etc.—its qualities and originality—least a priori of all theories—springs from actual and intimate acquaintance with emotions involved—Time and Free-will—Introduction à la Métaphysique— L'Effort Intellectuel—Laughter.

What exactly the theory does—statement of old theory in literary terms—then show how results of his system enable theory to be stated accurately—detailed demonstration of this difference—really fits closest to artist's own account.

How it answers (a) and (b).

In (b) his psychological results enable him to describe the indescribable process of artistic creation.

Defects of the theory—too much founded on analysis and experience of modern art—particularly symbolism—is this fatal?—amendments, no final criticism possible until his next book is published.

SPECULATIONS

His conception of Philosophy as an art.

The importance of art in his system, the key to the rest of his thought—no philosopher ever attached such importance to it.

Italian—Croce (Porena and Pilo)—not an empirical but a metaphysical æsthetic—part of a definite philosophical system—an account of it —its origins—its relation to Bergson's æsthetic— a criticism—relations to the German psychological systems.

CHAPTER 5.—*German* æsthetics : general account— general characteristics of the schools.

(*a*) the empirical school : *Vischer*, etc., modern experimental æsthetics, *Külpe, Neumann*, etc.

(*b*) the Einfühlung theories : *Lipps, Volkelt ;* history of the idea, Herder and the romantics.

(*c*) conscious-illusion theories—*Lange, Witasek ;*

(*d*) the historical, sociological school—Wundt, Schmarzow—art of *primitive people.*

CHAPTER 6.—*Lipps*—the greatest writer on æsthetics —the characteristics of his method—Vernon Lee's incorrect account of it ; What is Einfühlung ? The essential æsthetic phenomena—detailed application of the theory in Lipps' great book to— Form—Colour—Music—Tragedy—his theory of the comic.

CHAPTER 7.—*Lipps* (continued).

Comparison of the theory with the preceding ones—criticisms by the other German schools— final estimate.

CHAPTER 8.—The other German theories, more detailed account.

Formal æsthetics, *Cohen*, etc., and the Kantians.

CHAPTER 9.—Conclusions—How much definitely achieved—the problems still open. Future of the Subject.

APPENDIX C

AUTUMN

A touch of cold in the Autumn night—
I walked abroad,
And saw the ruddy moon lean over a hedge
Like a red-faced farmer.
I did not stop to speak, but nodded,
And round about were the wistful stars
With white faces like town children.

SPECULATIONS

MANA ABODA

*Beauty is the marking-time, the stationary
vibration, the feigned ecstasy of an arrested
impulse unable to reach its natural end.*

Mana Aboda, whose bent form
The sky in archèd circle is,
Seems ever for an unknown grief to mourn.
Yet on a day I heard her cry :
" I weary of the roses and the singing poets—
Josephs all, not tall enough to try."

ABOVE THE DOCK

Above the quiet dock in midnight,
Tangled in the tall mast's corded height,
Hangs the moon.   What seemed so far away
Is but a child's balloon, forgotten after play.

THE EMBANKMENT

*(The fantasia of a fallen gentleman on a cold,
bitter night.)*

Once, in finesse of fiddles found I ecstasy,
In a flash of gold heels on the hard pave-
    ment.
Now see I
That warmth's the very stuff of poesy.
Oh, God, make small
The old star-eaten blanket of the sky,
That I may fold it round me and in comfort
    lie.

CONVERSION

Light-hearted I walked into the valley wood
In the time of hyacinths,
Till beauty like a scented cloth
Cast over, stifled me.   I was bound
Motionless and faint of breath
By loveliness that is her own eunuch.

Now pass I to the final river
Ignominiously, in a sack, without sound,
As any peeping Turk to the Bosphorus.

INDEX

269

INDEX